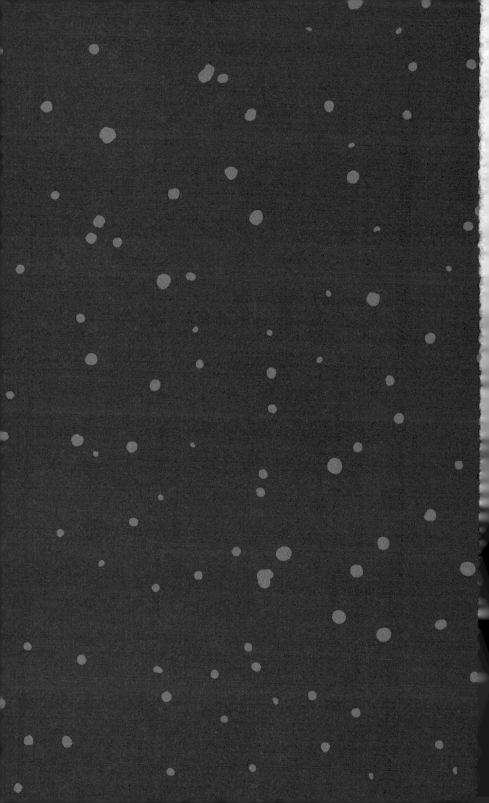

WITH ALL YOUR HEART

DEVOTIONS FOR GIRLS

KRISTI HOLL WITH JENNIFER VOGTLIN

 ZONDER**kidz**™

ZONDERKIDZ

With All Your Heart

Copyright © 2005 by Kristi Holl

Previously published as *Girlz Rock.*

Requests for information should be addressed to:
Zonderkidz, *3900 Sparks Dr. SE, Grand Rapids, Michigan 49546*

ISBN 978-0-310-12049-0 (hardcover)
ISBN 978-0-310-120-51-3 (ebook)

Cover Design: Michelle Lenger
Cover Art: istockphoto
Interior Design: Mallory Collins

Printed in India

21 22 23 24 25   RPI   10 9 8 7 6 5 4 3 2 1

Jesus replied: "'Love the Lord your God with all your heart and with all your soul and with all your mind.' This is the first and greatest commandment."

MATTHEW 22:37–38

DAY 1

THE NARROW ROAD

"Enter through the narrow gate. For wide is the gate and broad is the road that leads to destruction, and many enter through it. But small is the gate and narrow the road that leads to life, and only a few find it."

MATTHEW 7:13–14

You can enter God's kingdom only through the narrow gate that leads to life. The highway to hell is broad, and its gate is wide for the many who choose the easy way. But the road to life is narrow, and only a few ever find it.

Many of your friends will encourage you to join them on the wide path. It looks like fun, and Satan promises that you'll feel loved and accepted if you live as the world lives. You'll have more "friends" on the broad path. You won't be branded a "narrow-minded Christian" if you choose to travel on the Anything Goes Highway. On that wide path you'll hear that cheating to get good grades is okay, that R-rated movies don't hurt you, and that it's cool to drink and do drugs.

The broad way is also the way of disappointment and false promises. It can't deliver love and acceptance and long-lasting happiness because it's Satan's lie. Proverbs 16:25 (NKJV) says, "There is a way that seems right to a man, but its end is the way of death." The broad way might be fun for a while, but your heart will never find peace this way. True joy and acceptance are found through God on the narrow path. Traveling God's way can mean a difficult, rocky road at times. But it leads to peace here on earth and eternal life in heaven. It's not heavily traveled, but Jesus is always with you, so you're *never* alone.

You're standing at a fork in the road. Take off with confidence down the narrow way—to life!

REFLECTION QUESTIONS

What path are you walking on right now? Do you think God is happy with your choices?

_____

_____

_____

_____

PRAYER

Lord, I don't always make the right choices. Help me to be courageous and choose the right path. I want you to be proud of me. I love you. Amen.

DAY 2

Never-Ending Love

"The LORD appeared to us in the past, saying: 'I have loved you with an everlasting love; I have drawn you with unfailing kindness.'"

JEREMIAH 31:3

Our limited human minds find it hard to grasp how much God loves us. His love continues forever and can be counted on in all our times of need. God pulled us to him with his love and kindness. "We love Him because He first loved us" (1 John 4:19 NKJV).

Think about the person you love most in the world. Then multiply the love you feel for this person a thousand times. That's only a tiny drop of the love—the everlasting love—that God feels toward you.

Every day for the rest of this month, take a few minutes to think about how much God loves you. Say it out loud: "God loves *me*. The all-knowing, all-powerful, all-loving God of the universe loves *me*!" See how that changes your feelings during the month. We would live differently if we truly understood how much God loves us. He wants only the best for us—all the time. He wants to meet all our needs—we only have to ask him. (That doesn't mean he will give you everything you *want*, but instead everything he knows you need.) He wants to fight our battles for us—we only have to lean on him. He wants to give us direction and to have the joy Jesus died for us to have.

God wanted us so much that he pulled us to him. Jesus said, "No one can come to me unless the Father who sent me draws them" (John 6:44). People do not come to Christ strictly because of their own ideas or decisions. It is God pulling them to him. He loves you and wants you that much!

God's love for you is without limit. Soak it up!

REFLECTION QUESTIONS

Do you feel that God really loves you? How do you think he shows his love to you each day?

_____

_____

_____

_____

PRAYER

Lord, it's hard to believe that you love me so much, but I am so grateful to have your love. Help me to show love to others the way you show your love for me. Thank you for never leaving me. Amen.

Cultivate Your Faith

"Good soil represents those who hear and accept God's word and produce a harvest of thirty, sixty, or even a hundred times as much as had been planted!"

MARK 4:20 (NLT)

When you plant garden seeds, you don't expect much of a crop from dry, rocky ground, or a patch full of weeds. But good soil—black soil full of minerals—will produce up to a hundred times the amount of seed that was planted. In the same way, people with good hearts, ready to receive God's word and act on it, will also produce an abundant harvest. They will become all that God created them to be.

God has given you special talents and abilities that he wants you to use. Do you love to run fast? Do you have a good singing voice? Can you play an instrument, write poetry, or paint watercolors? God wants you to enjoy the gifts and talents, but also use them to bring joy to others and glory and praise to God. Is your life producing such a harvest? It can!

If you don't like your harvest, check your soil. Is it full of weeds (like resentment, laziness, or jealousy)? Then deal with the weeds. Pray for help to get rid of them, then do what God tells you to do. Is your soil dry and hard from lack of water (not reading your Bible)? Then soak it in the rivers of living water from

God's Word. Then you'll grow the fruit of the Spirit: love, joy, peace, patience, kindness, goodness, faithfulness, gentleness, and self-control (Galatians 5:22–23 NLT).

If your soil needs attention, be a good farmer and plow it. Plant it with seeds of obedience to God's Word—then reap your harvest!

Reflection Questions

Are you using your talents to the best of your abilities? Can others see God's influence in your behavior?

_____

_____

_____

_____

Prayer

Lord, I want to use my talents for you. Please help me to honor you in all I do. I want to produce a good harvest! Amen.

The Popular Group

"Don't boast about following a particular human leader. For
everything belongs to you."

1 CORINTHIANS 3:21 (NLT)

Don't get your feelings of self-respect or personal worth from
being accepted by a particular person or group. Because you
belong to Christ, they don't have anything that you don't have!

Most classes have a few girls who have decided they are the
popular group. They will claim to have inside information that
others don't have, or act as if they are more special than anyone
else. Don't fall for that! Don't believe the lie that claims you have
to be part of someone's group to be cool. You already belong to
the coolest group you could join: Father, Son, and Holy Spirit!

God designed you to have friendships that are rewarding,
with give-and-take sharing. Relationships get out of balance when
one person thinks she's better than others. YOU are important,
valuable, and significant. Centering your life on someone who
demands to be the focus will throw your friendship out of balance.

If you belong to Christ (have accepted him as your Savior),
then you're a daughter of the King. Everything God has belongs
to Christ, and everything Jesus has is yours. If you stay true to
him, all the blessings here and in eternity belong to you. You
are as worthy as anyone else on earth—anyone! So don't brag

about being part of a particular group, or follow the popular girls because they have more of what the world offers. God says you have worth and value. You are worth so much to him that he sent his Son to die for you so that you could spend eternity with him. You can't get any more valuable than that!

REFLECTION QUESTIONS

Where do you go to feel wanted and respected? Do you rely on friends for self-esteem or God?

_____

_____

_____

_____

PRAYER

Lord, I sometimes worry too much about what others think of me. Please help me remember that you are the one I need to please. In you, I have all the love and respect I will ever need! Thank you! Amen.

DAY 5

BE A GOD PLEASER

"Obviously, I'm not trying to win the approval of people, but of God. If pleasing people were my goal, I would not be Christ's servant."

GALATIANS 1:10 (NLT)

Are you trying to win the approval and acceptance of people? Is that your primary reason for saying and doing things? You can't spend your time trying to win the approval of people and still be a servant of Christ.

At the lunch table, when someone tells a dirty joke, do you laugh too so you'll be accepted, even when the joke makes you very uncomfortable? Or do you gossip about other students so you won't feel left out, even though you know it's wrong? Do you ignore a less popular student because your friends would make fun of you if you were nice to him? Then you are trying to please people instead of pleasing God. And God's Word says you can't be in God's service—useful to him—if you're more interested in people's opinions than God's opinion.

As believers, we are to be like Christ and follow in his foot-steps. How did he handle such situations? Once the Pharisees tried to trap Jesus into saying something they could use against him. "'Teacher,' they said, 'we know you are a man of integrity and that you teach the way of God in accordance with the truth.

You aren't swayed by others, because you pay no attention to who they are'" (Matthew 22:16). Jesus didn't play favorites or change what he said depending on who was listening. He said and did what God told him to say and do, no matter whom he was around. We are to do the same.

Go out and live your life today in a way that pleases God.

Reflection Questions

When you think about doing something, do you only worry about others' reactions? Or do you also think about what God would say?

_____

_____

_____

_____

Prayer

Lord, I'm not always proud of the way I act, and I need your forgiveness. Help me to do what you would do, at all times. I want to be a great witness for you! Amen.

DAY 6

LIVING IN LOVE

"As the Father has loved me, so have I loved you. Now remain in my love."

JOHN 15:9

Jesus wants you to know how much he loves you. Jesus said that he loves you just as God, the Father, loves him. Just as much, and in the same way. Imagine that! So it's important that you continue to rest and live in that everlasting, bountiful love.

Sometimes it's hard to believe God can love us that much. After all, we all do things that we know are wrong and for which we need forgiveness. Maybe you cheated and turned in an assignment that you copied off a friend. Perhaps you pretend to like your stepmother, but you secretly hate her. When you're so imperfect, can God still love you? YES! Or maybe your family is breaking up, or your mental health is breaking down. Does God still love you, no matter what is happening in your life? YES! "I am convinced that nothing can ever separate us from God's love. Neither death nor life, neither angels nor demons, neither our fears for today nor our worries about tomorrow—not even the powers of hell can separate us from God's love" (Romans 8:38 NLT).

Sometimes we need reminders that God loves us. Say it out loud: "God loves me, and I can trust him. God loves me, and I can trust him." If you have trouble believing that God really cares about you or that he can forgive you for your sins, repeat that to yourself several times a day for a month. Get it down deep inside you. In time, your love for others will also grow. "God is love, and all who live in love live in God, and God lives in them. And as we live in God, our love grows more perfect" (1 John 4:16–17 NLT).

Settle down, get comfortable, relax—and live in God's love for you.

Reflection Questions

Do you have days when you think that God can't possibly love you? Would it help to remind yourself daily that God *does* love you?

_____

_____

_____

_____

Prayer

Lord, I know you love me so much that I can't understand it. Sometimes, I can't even believe it. Please help me to remember every day that you love me. Thank you for your love that never ends. Amen.

YOUR PERSONAL BODYGUARD

"So we say with confidence, 'The Lord is my helper; I will not
be afraid. What can mere mortals do to me?'"

HEBREWS 13:6

As we look at events in our lives, God's Word says that we can
be confident. Why? Because the almighty, all-loving Lord is our
helper. So we don't need to be worried or insecure. With the all-
powerful God on our side, what can people do to us?

Bullies are a nasty reality of life sometimes. A bully may be
an older sibling who dominates the house when your parents are
at work. It can be a teacher or coach who discourages you with
their comments. Maybe it's a brutal kid mocking you in school
or on social media. Life can be *scary* sometimes.

We may think bullies are a modern thing. We might even think
that God doesn't understand our situation. But bullies have been
around for thousands of years! Look at David's words in the Psalms:

> "In God (I will praise His word),
> In God I have put my trust;
> I will not fear.
> What can flesh do to me?
> All day they twist my words;
> All their thoughts are against me for evil.

They gather together,
They hide, they mark my steps,
When they lie in wait for my life."

PSALM 56:4–6 NKJV

You may be powerless to deal with them on your own, but with God on your side, you don't have to be afraid. Go to God in prayer. "Let us therefore come boldly to the throne of grace, that we may obtain mercy and find grace to help in time of need" (Hebrews 4:16 NKJV).

Pray. Believe. Watch. Say boldly, "I will not fear!"

REFLECTION QUESTIONS

Do you ever feel bullied by others? Have you ever asked God to deliver you from them?

_____

_____

_____

_____

PRAYER

Lord, sometimes other people try to scare me. You are my rock and my refuge. Please deliver me from their words and actions. Thank you. Amen.

Strength Training for Your Spirit

"The spirit of a man sustains him in sickness,
But as for a broken spirit, who can bear it?"

PROVERBS 18:14 (AMP)

Everyone will experience sickness or trouble sometimes, but if your spirit is strong, you can face it and survive. But someone with a weak or wounded spirit finds it nearly impossible to bear up under anything. Their problems may not be worse than anyone else's, but they won't be strong enough to endure or overcome their difficulties.

Haven't you noticed this difference in yourself? On Monday, when you're confident inside and someone calls you a stupid name, you shrug it off. You know that the problem is with the other person, not you. But if it happens again on Wednesday, when you feel weaker inside, the same remark makes you cry. Sometimes you know why you're feeling down (a bad grade, a fight with a friend, the flu), but some days there seems to be no reason. When your spirit is weak, it's hard to overcome or endure anything with the right attitude.

So what can you do? First, you must learn to encourage yourself. There won't always be someone around to do it for you. David learned this too and wrote, "Why, my soul, are you downcast? Why so disturbed within me? Put your hope in God, for I will yet praise him, my Savior and my God" (Psalm 42:11). He talked to himself! He said, "What's the matter with you? Why are you down in the dumps? Put your hope in God, not these circumstances!" David had learned to encourage himself.

You should also encourage others when you see that they need a kind or uplifting word. Be the kind of girl people love to see coming because they feel better every time you're around. "Encourage the disheartened, help the weak, be patient with everyone" (1 Thessalonians 5:14).

Be strong in spirit, and you can handle anything!

Reflection Questions

Are there days when your spirit feels stronger and more confident? Or weaker and easily hurt? Do you ask God for help?

Prayer

Lord, sometimes my spirit gets hurt so easily.
Please help me to rely on you, not on others.
I want my hope to stay in you! Amen.

How to Stay Calm, No Matter What

"Blessed is the one you discipline, Lord,
the one you teach from your law;
you grant them relief from days of trouble,
till a pit is dug for the wicked."

PSALM 94:12–13

The person whom God corrects, trains, and teaches is happy and very fortunate. This person is given rest and relief from troubled times. God gives him the "[power to calm himself and find] peace in the days of adversity" (Psalm 94:13 AMP).

Some problems are over quickly, but some seem to drag on and on. Maybe your mom has a serious illness that requires medical attention. Or you have an older brother who embarrasses you. You want relief from your day of trouble—and the ability to be at peace until it's over.

Wouldn't you *love* to have the power to stay calm, no matter what happened? You can have this power! Just don't miss the part that has to come first. Before the power comes, God uses the events and people in our lives to build our spiritual character. For example, he may teach you about the power of prayer during your mom's illness. He wants us to be calm and steadfast. After being taught by God, we become stable, happy, and powerful. Then we can remain calm and steady while we wait for our troubles to work out.

Why is God's discipline good? (It sure doesn't FEEL good sometimes!) This is what David said about it: "I used to wander off until you disciplined me; but now I closely follow your word. You are good and do only good; teach me your decrees" (Psalm 119:67–68 NLT).

God's discipline keeps you on the narrow path, where he knows the biggest blessings—like peace and happiness—await you.

Reflection Questions

When you face problems, do you want them to be over right away? Have you ever thought that God allows problems because he loves you?

_____

_____

_____

_____

Prayer

Lord, it's hard to wait for my problems to be over. Help me to remember that you send trials my way in order for me to grow. Thank you for loving me so much! Amen.

BE BUSY, NOT A BUSYBODY

"Make it your ambition to lead a quiet life: You should mind
your own business and work with your hands, just as we told
you."

I THESSALONIANS 4:11

We all want to lead a life that is free from turmoil. We want to
be calm and well-balanced. Paul says that one way to do this is
by paying attention to (and taking care of) your own business.
Don't go poking your nose into other people's personal matters.

When friends ask you something a little too personal, like
how much you paid for something, how much you weigh, or who
you have a crush on, you want to say, "Hey, mind your own business!" Feel free, in a kind tone of voice, to say just that. People
need to pay attention to their own concerns instead of gossiping
about other people's business. (If you want to tell your friends
a private detail, that's one thing. But they *don't* have a right to
know just because they are nosy enough to ask.) It goes both
ways too. No matter how curious you feel about another person's
private life, mind your own business and focus on your own life.

The Greeks felt that manual labor (working with your hands)
was degrading and only for slaves. But the Bible makes it clear
that all honest work is godly. If you're working hard on the things
you need to do, you won't have time to be nosy. "We hear that

some among you are idle and disruptive. They are not busy; they are busybodies" (2 Thessalonians 3:11). Idleness (not working) often leads to this problem. People who are paying attention to their own jobs, families, schoolwork, and church activities rarely have time to be nosy.

Let other people mind their own affairs while you pay attention to yours. Everyone will benefit!

REFLECTION QUESTIONS

When you are with your friends or classmates, can you be open with them? Do they try to find out every private thing about you? If so, what could you say to them?

_____

_____

_____

_____

PRAYER

Lord, I thank you that I have friends who are interested in me. Please help me tell the difference between true caring and prying. I want to have true friends and be one myself. Thank you. Amen.

Promises Worth Waiting For

"You need to persevere so that when you have done the will of God, you will receive what he has promised."

HEBREWS 10:36

You need to have patience and stick to your plan of action, no matter how long something takes. Why? So that (after you have done what God commanded) you will receive all of what he promised to give you.

TV shows, movies, and magazines cry, "Get it now!" It might be an instant meal, instant cash, or instant beauty. God's Word says the opposite. He gives a specific promise and tells you how to obtain it. But after you've done what God said, there's usually a waiting period before the promise appears. God uses that waiting period to "grow you up" spiritually, developing character qualities that will benefit you all your life.

What things has God promised to give believers? Everything from love and peace to eternal life. He also gives us wise principles to live by. For example, if you need money, check out these ideas (and see what God tells *you* to do): "A generous person will prosper; whoever refreshes others will be refreshed" (Proverbs 11:25). And "Whoever sows generously will also reap generously" (2 Corinthians 9:6). And "All hard work brings a profit, but mere talk leads only to poverty" (Proverbs 14:23). Your part? Work hard and be generous. Be persistent. Practicing these principles over time can turn your circumstances around.

Being patient is *not* the ability to sit calmly and do nothing, waiting for something to happen. Patient perseverance, the kind needed to receive God's promises, is very active. It's hanging tough when it gets hard, when you want to take a shortcut to get what you want.

Instead, "Rest in the Lord, and wait patiently for Him" (Psalm 37:7 NKJV). Your promise is on its way!

Reflection Questions

Is it hard for you to wait for something you want or need? Do you talk to God about it?

_____

_____

_____

_____

Prayer

Lord, it's hard for me to be patient. Help me to remember that the answer is on its way. Thank you for meeting my needs. Amen.

Uncommon Common Sense

"Only simpletons believe everything they're told!
The prudent carefully consider their steps."

PROVERBS 14:15 (NLT)

Some people lack common sense. These inexperienced people will believe anything they're told and follow along blindly. A wise, sensible person, however, shows good judgment and self-control. This person gives very careful thought before taking any action.

How many times have you wrongly believed or trusted someone? Maybe they promised they'd pay you back the money you loaned them but never did. Or asked for "help" with their math homework, but expected you to give them all the answers. Or maybe you found out that a so-called friend was talking about you behind your back.

Sometimes we mistakenly think that it's not Christian to doubt someone's word or question things we're told. We've read that being suspicious is a sin, so we hide our misgivings and give the other person the benefit of the doubt. But believing everything you're told is a good way to get into trouble. Instead, you must find a balance. If something sounds fishy or too good to be true, take a step back, because it probably is. You don't have to snarl, "I know you're lying!" (That's not speaking the truth in love.) But don't agree too quickly either, and don't make commitments you'll regret later. Always talk to the Lord about your misgivings and those funny feelings in the pit of your stomach. The Holy Spirit may be trying to get your attention so you can steer clear of danger or avoid making a bad decision. Romans 16:17–18 (NKJV) says to "avoid . . . those who . . . by smooth words and flattering speech deceive the hearts of the simple."

Be wise. Examine what people tell you. Then give careful thought to what you should do.

REFLECTION QUESTIONS

Do you tend to believe everything you're told? Do you ask questions and try to find out the real story? Do you ever get that funny feeling in your stomach telling you something's not right?

PRAYER

Lord, I'm glad that I have friends to talk with.
Please give me wisdom to know who is truthful
and to avoid those who lie. Help me to be
truthful at all times. Thank you. Amen.

THE HEART OF THE MATTER

"A good man brings good things out of the good stored up in his heart, and an evil man brings evil things out of the evil stored up in his heart. For the mouth speaks what the heart is full of."

LUKE 6:45

Whatever is truly in your heart will come out in your words and actions. You can't pretend for long. If you have a heart full of good, you'll do and say good things. If someone's words and actions are unkind, it's because they have evil stored in their heart instead. Whatever is in your heart determines what you say.

When your little brother chatters nonstop on the way to school, do you tell him to shut up, or do you say, "That sounds interesting"? When your friends are gossiping at lunch, do you join in or find something positive to say? Whatever comes out of your mouth reveals the condition of your heart.

There shouldn't be a mixture—some good, some bad—coming out of our mouths, but oftentimes there is. Even if 90 percent of what you say is positive and good, there might be a particular person or situation that continually tempts you to say things that aren't godly. If so, take the matter to God. Ask him to reveal whatever unforgiving thoughts and feelings live in your heart, and deal with them. Read Psalm 51, and confess whatever needs confessing. "Create in me a pure heart, O God, and renew a steadfast spirit within me" (v. 10). Your mouth is like a barometer of your heart, measuring and revealing its condition, so pay attention to your words.

Feed your heart a steady diet of the Word of God. Then watch your mouth become a fountain of blessings for everyone you meet!

· REFLECTION QUESTIONS

Do you watch the words that come out of your mouth? What situations are the hardest for you?

_____

_____

_____

_____

PRAYER

Lord, I have good intentions, but I don't always say nice things. Please help me to think before I speak. I want to say what you would say. Thank you! Amen.

GOD USES PROBLEMS TO DIRECT YOU

"No discipline seems pleasant at the time, but painful. Later on, however, it produces a harvest of righteousness and peace for those who have been trained by it."

HEBREWS 12:11

We don't enjoy discipline while it's happening—it's painful! Being trained in self-control is hard! But afterward, you will have peace and the blessings of right living reserved for those who let these experiences train them.

It wasn't until Morgan bought new school clothes that she realized she had not watched her nutrition like she should have over the summer. Returning to school was difficult. She got winded climbing stairs and in gym class. Worst of all, she couldn't finish her gymnastics workouts and eventually got dropped from the team.

Discipline often comes in the form of problems we want to hide from. We often fail to see how God is trying to use *those very problems* to help us learn more about ourselves. Take time to pray and consider how God might be using that problem to benefit you. Remember that "the Lord disciplines the one he loves" (Hebrews 12:6), and "God disciplines us for our good" (Hebrews 12:10).

Sometimes it takes a painful situation for God to get our attention. He may want to turn you in a different direction or motivate you to make a change in your life. Losing her place on the gymnastics team was painful for Morgan. However, it motivated her to look more carefully after her body, which is the temple of the Holy Spirit.

Developing self-control is hard, but remember the rewards! Stay focused on the prize you'll receive at the end.

Reflection Questions

How do you handle being disciplined? Can you understand why you need to be corrected from time to time? Do you see why God wants to correct you?

_____

_____

_____

_____

Prayer

Lord, being corrected is not my favorite thing. I usually get really upset. Please help me to remember that you discipline me because you love me. You want what is best for me. Thank you for loving me that much! Amen.

God Uses Problems to Inspect You

"Consider it pure joy, my brothers and sisters, whenever you face trials of many kinds, because you know that the testing of your faith produces perseverance."

JAMES 1:2–3

Whenever trouble of any kind comes your way, let it be an opportunity for joy. Problems test our faith to see what it's really made of. Problems and tests also give our endurance and patience a chance to grow. It's easy to believe we trust God, and to look like our faith is strong, when we don't have any problems. But problems test our faith and reveal what's really inside us.

People are like tea bags. If you want to know what's inside, drop them into hot water! Your faith is like that, too. When faced with a problem—an angry parent or friend, a sprained ankle before the track meet—how's your faith? Are you still confident that God will meet all your needs? Do you wait patiently for God's answers and help? Until you've seen God supply your needs and help you through a few problems, it can be extremely hard to view problems as opportunities for joy. But "blessed is the one who perseveres under trial because, having stood the test, that person will receive the crown of life that the Lord has promised to those who love him" (James 1:12). Once your faith has endured a few tests, you will view problems differently. You will know a blessing waits for you after you face the trial successfully. Usually, the bigger the test, the bigger the reward for keeping your faith in God strong.

Whatever trial or problem you're facing today, thank God for the opportunity to grow stronger in your faith. Keep trusting God, and it will happen!

REFLECTION QUESTIONS

Have you ever thought of problems as a chance to grow? Do you stay close to God during trials?

_____

_____

_____

_____

PRAYER

Lord, I am learning that trials are a chance to grow
in my faith. Please help me to remember that.
Thank you for always being with me. Amen.

GOD USES PROBLEMS TO CONNECT YOU

"My suffering was good for me,
for it taught me to pay attention to your decrees."

PSALM 119:71 (NLT)

Pain hurts at the time we feel it, but it's good for us if it teaches us to pay attention to God's rules for our personal behavior. Unhappiness and distress feel bad, but when the suffering teaches us something as valuable as God's rules for living, the pain is a blessing in disguise.

Anna refused to wear her helmet; then she received a concussion when her bike crashed. Sarah talked on the phone until midnight on school nights, then was so exhausted, she missed a trip to the water park. Kate went to the mall when she was supposed to be studying, so she failed several tests.

Each girl had plenty of problems and pain to work through, but (in the end) Anna began wearing her helmet, Sarah started getting enough sleep, and Kate studied during the school week instead of shopping. Their lives were much more successful. Their problems were blessings in disguise.

Some lessons we learn only through pain and failure.

Sometimes, unfortunately, we only learn the true value of something—health, money, friendship—by losing it, at least long enough to feel some pain. "I used to wander off until you disciplined me; but now I closely follow your word. You are good and do only good; teach me your decrees" (Psalm 119:67–68 NLT).

The next time you face a problem, pray and ask God if he is trying to teach you something. Listen for his answer. Then obey yourself right out of the problem!

REFLECTION QUESTIONS

Think back to a time when you made a wrong choice. What were the consequences? Do you think God was teaching you something?

_____

_____

_____

_____

PRAYER

Lord, I sometimes make sinful and unwise choices.
Please help me to see what I did wrong, so that I don't
do it again. I want to learn and grow. Amen.

DAY 17

GOD USES PROBLEMS TO PROTECT YOU

"You intended to harm me, but God intended it for good to accomplish what is now being done, the saving of many lives."

GENESIS 50:20

As far as Joseph was concerned, God turned into good what his brothers meant for evil. Joseph's brothers, out of jealousy, sold him into slavery. But God used their betrayal to put Joseph in a place of power in Egypt. God brought Joseph to that high position so he could save the lives of many people during a famine when there was a severe shortage of food. God brought good out of the evil. He still works like this in the lives of believers.

Jenny's feelings were terribly hurt when her best friend dumped her because Jenny wouldn't shoplift a bracelet "just for fun." Six months later, Jenny was grateful to God that she wasn't at the mall with her friend when she was arrested for theft. The friendship was broken to protect Jenny.

Alyssa was hurt that her parents didn't seem to trust her—they wouldn't let her ride to school with the teenage neighbor boy. But when he totaled his car while speeding, Alyssa was grateful that God used her parents' *No!* to protect her.

Sometimes we have friendship problems, and no matter

what we do, the friendship dies. Perhaps God knows that down the road, being friends with that person would do us more harm than good. God used Joseph's painful situation (being sold into slavery) to save him and many others from a worse problem: dying from hunger.

So when you face a problem or a disappointment, take time to pray. Ask God if he is perhaps trying to protect you from serious pain in the future. Then give him your thanks and praise!

Reflection Questions

When you look back at your past problems, did God do you a favor by allowing some trouble into your life? Can you see any results now that you couldn't see then?

_____

_____

_____

_____

Prayer

Lord, I sometimes don't understand why you allow problems to come my way. Please help me to know whether you are trying to protect me. Thank you for your perfect wisdom in my life. Amen.

GOD USES PROBLEMS TO PERFECT YOU

"We can rejoice, too, when we run into problems and trials, for we know that they help us develop endurance. And endurance develops strength of character, and character strengthens our confident hope of salvation."

ROMANS 5:3–4 (NLT)

We can have joy even in the middle of problems and pain. We aren't happy *because* we have problems, but because we know suffering has a purpose. Part of God's purpose is to produce character in his children. And he knows that problems help us learn to hang in there when things are hard. This endurance builds strong qualities that will help us make good decisions in life. However, remember that the problems themselves don't build character. *Responding correctly* to problems is what develops a godly character.

Beth and Rosa both had mean stepfathers they didn't like. Rosa got into yelling matches with him and ended up running away from home. Beth's stepfather was just as difficult, but she chose to respond differently. She knew that God's Word says, "Love your enemies! Pray for those who persecute you!" (Matthew 5:44 NLT). Beth decided to pray for her stepfather's heart to be softened. It didn't happen overnight—it took endurance on Beth's part—but within a year she and her stepfather were spending time together fishing. Beth chose to allow her problem to help her grow.

We start out as spiritual babies, and we need to grow up. If we always got everything we wanted, we'd be spoiled and remain babies. For that reason, God allows problems and trials into our lives.

The next time you face a problem, be determined to learn from it. Let God use it to perfect your character.

Reflection Questions

Think of a problem you are facing now, whether big or small. If you didn't know about God's Word, what would you do about the problem? How would God say to respond?

_____

_____

_____

_____

Prayer

Lord, I want to do what you would do when a problem comes my way. Help me to remember you are testing me to make my faith grow. Thank you for loving me. Amen.

DAY 19

ILLUMINATING YOUR LIFE

"Your word is a lamp to guide my feet,
and a light for my path."

PSALM 119:105 (NLT)

We're all on a journey through life. It can be dark and confusing at times. But God's Word—the principles and commandments in it—light the way. It makes the narrow path visible, so we don't have to stumble and fall. Lamps and lights also serve as warning signals, like when a bridge is out. In the same manner, God's Word acts as a signal, warning us away from trouble.

Amber is a new girl in the sixth grade who wants to make friends. Should she choose the plain girl who is calm and kind, or the flashy, fun-looking girl with a short temper? If Amber looks in God's Word, it will shine a light on her path. "Do not make friends with a hot-tempered person, do not associate with one easily angered" (Proverbs 22:24). How about Heather? She doesn't know how to handle a bully in her gym class. If she wants to make a wise decision, she'll let God's Word shine a light on her situation. "Fools shows their annoyance at once, but the prudent overlook an insult" (Proverbs 12:16).

Maybe you can't find a specific Bible verse to cover your situation. If not, pray and ask God for his advice. He promises to give it to you. James 1:5 (NLT) says, "If you need wisdom, ask our generous God, and he will give it to you. He will not rebuke you for asking." Sometimes you can sense the answer right away, and sometimes you have to wait for a while before you know what to do. But God *will* answer. "You will light my lamp; the LORD my God will enlighten my darkness" (Psalm 18:28 NKJV).

Put an end to the darkness on your path through life. Turn on the Light!

REFLECTION QUESTIONS

When you have a problem, do you do what you want to do? Or do you ask God what he wants you to do?

_____

_____

_____

_____

PRAYER

Lord, I don't always wait for you to tell me
what to do. Help me to stop and pray about my
problems before I do anything. I know what
you want for me is best. Thank you. Amen.

DAY 20

STAND STRONG

"The temptations in your life are no different from what others experience. And God is faithful. He will not allow the temptation to be more than you can stand. When you are tempted, he will show you a way out so that you can endure."

1 CORINTHIANS 10:13 (NLT)

We all want to have—or do—something that we know we should avoid. Everyone experiences temptation of one kind or another, and the temptation itself is NOT a sin. It's only a test. God is always there for you. Turn to him, and ask for help. God won't let the test, or temptation, get too strong for you to fight. He will show you a way out so you don't have to give in to it.

Temptations come in all shapes and sizes. Your older sister left her wallet on the table, and she probably won't notice if you take a little of her money. Your friend hurt you, and you suddenly want to gossip about her to anyone who will listen. The Bible says that temptations happen to all people. God won't shield you from all temptation, but he won't let it overpower you. He'll give you a way out if you really want to overcome it.

Sometimes you need to get away from the temptation. If you're tempted by something you can't afford, leave the store. If you're tempted to take some money, remember these words and get away: "The love of money is a root of all kinds of evil, for which some have strayed from the faith in their greediness...But you, O man of God, flee these things and pursue righteousness, godliness, faith, love, patience, gentleness" (1 Timothy 6:10–11 NKJV). No matter what test you face, God will be faithful in each and every one. He'll show you a way out.

So stand strong in the Lord!

Reflection Questions

What are some things that tempt you? What do you do when they are staring you in the face? What do you think God wants you to do?

_____

_____

_____

_____

Prayer

Lord, sometimes I feel really tempted. I know I should avoid it, but it's hard to resist. Help me to resist temptation and rely on you for all my needs. Thank you for never leaving my side! Amen.

DEALING WITH DISAPPOINTMENT

"The sisters sent word to Jesus, 'Lord, the one you love is sick.' When he heard this, Jesus said, 'This sickness will not end in death. No, it is for God's glory so that God's Son may be glorified through it.'"

JOHN 11:3–4

Martha, Mary, and their brother (Lazarus) were Jesus' very close friends. So when they sent urgent word to Jesus that Lazarus was deathly sick, they were terribly disappointed and hurt when Jesus didn't hurry to their home and heal him.

Jesus loved them, but he waited two days to respond. Mary and Martha had no idea that God was planning something even greater than healing Lazarus. He was going to raise him from the dead!

We all are disappointed at times by those we love. Caitlin's best friend promised to stay overnight on Friday, but she forgot and went shopping with her sister instead. Nicole asked her dad for help on her science project, but by the time he was available, the deadline was past. Samantha prayed that they wouldn't have to move, but her mom got transferred anyway.

We need to remember that God knows more about every situation than we do. When we are very disappointed, we need to remind ourselves that God knows *everything*. It's like we're standing on a street corner, watching a parade. We can only see the float or band that's right in front of us. But God is like the TV cameraman high up on the corner of the roof who can see the whole parade: beginning, middle, and end. Mary and Martha could only see that their brother had died. But Jesus knew the ending—that he was going to raise Lazarus from the dead and display God's power.

The next time you're disappointed, trust that God knows more about the situation than you do. He has a much better plan in mind!

REFLECTION QUESTIONS

Who has disappointed you in the recent past? Did you rely on yourself (or on God) to cheer up? Have you disappointed anyone lately? If so, have you asked for forgiveness?

_____

_____

_____

_____

PRAYER

Lord, sometimes I feel hurt by the way others treat me. Help me to let go of my hurt feelings and to rely on you for my happiness. Thank you for never failing me! Amen.

FIGHTING BACK WITH · · · PRAYER?

"They surround me with hateful words
and fight against me for no reason.
I love them, but they try to destroy me with accusations
even as I am praying for them!"

PSALM 109:3–4 (NLT)

Sometimes, for no reason, people will make up lies about you. People like to slander and gossip, and you may be the target sometimes. Even when you treat them right, they may be hateful in return. Your response to that? Pray to God about the situation, but also pray for them.

Heather couldn't understand why the girls in her gym class chose to ridicule her. Heather wasn't any different than anyone else. Maria's own mother attacked her with hateful words too—at home. Her mom was miserable at work and going through a divorce; no matter how hard Maria tried, her mom poured out her anger and frustration on Maria. Heather decided to fight back, and the situation worsened as the girls bullied her even more. Maria prayed nightly instead, and God comforted her, even though her mom didn't change for months.

Even when you are trying to do everything right, there may be some people in your life who are nasty and hateful, slandering you for no reason. It can be classmates, kids at church, even people within your own family. It's very sad, but it does sometimes happen. The psalmist said he loved and prayed for those mean-spirited people, but they fought him anyway.

Why does it happen? Sometimes others can misunderstand the things you do. And you can't please people all the time, no matter how hard you try. Instead, do what you believe will please *God* and is right in his eyes. Then pray about any bad, hateful reactions you get from others.

No matter how others act, choose to show them love and pray for them. God will richly bless you for it.

Reflection Questions

Are there any people in your life who are determined to be nasty? How do you respond? Do you fight back or rely on God?

_____

_____

_____

_____

Prayer

Lord, I try to do the right thing, but sometimes people are hateful anyway. I want to respond the way Jesus would. Help me to focus on you and not on fighting back. Thank you. Amen.

DON'T LOSE YOURSELF

"Do not be misled: 'Bad company corrupts good character.'"

I CORINTHIANS 15:33

Don't be fooled into thinking that it doesn't matter what kinds of friends you have. Hanging out with immoral and dishonest friends can change you! They can ruin your good habits, morals, and godly character.

Megan's mom was worried about the new friends Megan made at school. Two of the girls were constantly in the principal's office for disrupting class. One friend had been suspended for shoplifting. Megan assured her mom that she'd never do such things, and she was telling the truth. She honestly had no intention of becoming like those girls. A few months later, Megan was using the same bad language at school and occupying her own seat in the principal's office.

Sometimes believers think that they can hang out with dishonest or immoral friends because Jesus did it. After all, he hung out with thieving tax collectors and prostitutes. Shouldn't we do the same thing so that we can be good witnesses to them? Yes, and no. There is a difference between talking with "bad company" and choosing them for your closest friends.

Consider this example. When you mix a glass of pure, clean water with a glass of dirty water, it all becomes dirty and cloudy.

The dirt spreads—not the purity. If you're healthy when you sit next to a very sick person, you can catch his flu, but he won't catch your health. In the same way, bad habits and behavior are contagious.

It's good to be friendly with everyone, but choose moral girls with good character for your closest friends. Then you can build one another up and grow spiritually together.

Reflection Questions

Who are your closest friends? How do they behave? How do you behave when you are with them?

_____

_____

_____

_____

Prayer

Lord, I want to make good choices when making friends.
Help me to find those who have good character and
who want to get closer to you. Thank you. Amen.

DAY 24

FIND A WAY TO FORGIVE

"Make allowance for each other's faults, and forgive anyone who offends you. Remember, the Lord forgave you, so you must forgive others."

COLOSSIANS 3:13 (NLT)

You need to patiently put up with others' faults. Forgive any grudges or resentments you're carrying about another person. Remember how much the Lord has forgiven you! As Christians, we are expected to do likewise and forgive others.

We often have to forgive our family members for their faults many times each week. Maybe your dad is forgetful, and he doesn't remember your birthday until he sees the cake on the supper table. Your sister likes to gossip, and she tells her boyfriend about the test you failed. Your little brother is clumsy, and he spills soda all over your new jacket. We can't help but make mistakes sometimes, but one thing we can control is letting go of our anger and offering forgiveness.

Forgiving someone—letting them off the hook—often has to be an act of will. If you wait till you *feel* like forgiving someone, you may never do it. And we are commanded to forgive. God would not command us to do something if it were impossible to do. Forgiveness is real the moment we choose to forgive, but it can take weeks or months for our feelings to change, depending on how big the hurt is.

True forgiveness can make a positive impact on the forgiven person. Without it, bitterness and hurt feelings grow even stronger. Forgiving another person does not mean you're saying what they did was okay. But it DOES mean that you are committed to moving past it. Revenge and hatred may hurt others, but they are more likely to destroy *you*.

Be patient, and cultivate the forgiving habit. Then watch the peace and joy grow in your own heart.

REFLECTION QUESTIONS

Is there someone you need to forgive? Are you willing to give up your hurt feelings toward them? Are you ready to move on?

_____

_____

_____

_____

PRAYER

Lord, it's really hard, but today I'm going to choose to forgiveness. I don't want to be bitter anymore. Please help me to really forgive and get on with my life. Thank you for your willingness to always forgive me. Amen.

DAY 25

STRENGTH FROM WITHIN

"I pray that out of his glorious riches he may strengthen you
with power through his Spirit in your inner being, so that
Christ may dwell in your hearts through faith."

EPHESIANS 3:16–17

Others often disappoint us, and we also disappoint God. At other
times we're sick or we're just plain tired. We wonder if we can go
on. Maybe not—in our *own* strength. But God has an unlimited
supply of strength available to those who have trusted in Christ.

Kylie ate a whole box of cookies, after promising herself she'd
eat just two. She was so tired of trying to lose the weight her
doctor suggested. Amber was disappointed too, but in her mom.
She'd promised *again* to make it to her soccer game, but when
Amber scored the winning goal, her mom wasn't there to see
it—*again*. Amber felt like giving up. What can these girls do for
strength when their own has run out? As believers, they can pray
for help. "In the day when I cried out, You answered me, And
made me bold with strength in my soul" (Psalm 138:3 NKJV).

Whenever we experience a disappointment, we need to be
refreshed and encouraged. As you trust in God more and more,
Jesus will be more and more "at home" in your heart. When that
happens, your disappointments won't seem like such a big deal
because you'll know you're not alone. Even more than God wants

to remove your pain or uncomfortable circumstances, he wants to use them first to help you grow.

Instead of focusing on negative circumstances on the outside, pray for God to strengthen you on the inside. He will!

REFLECTION QUESTIONS

Think about the last time you were disappointed. Did you dwell on how bad things were for you? Did you ask God for help and encouragement?

_____

_____

_____

_____

PRAYER

Lord, sometimes I feel too weak to keep going
every day. Please help me to remember that
you will give me all the strength I need. Thank
you for always being here for me. Amen.

DAY 26

RUNNING FOR YOUR LIFE

"Do you not know that in a race all the runners run, but only
one gets the prize? Run in such a way as to get the prize."

I CORINTHIANS 9:24

Believers are like runners in a race. In order to finish well, runners
have to focus on the finish line. Heaven is the finish line for believers. If you want to live a life that counts, that has purpose, you need
to live today while keeping the future in mind at all times.

June had accepted Christ as her Savior two summers before
at church camp. For more than a year, she read her Bible daily,
talked to her friends about Jesus, faithfully attended Sunday
school, and was careful to choose godly friends. When she went
to middle school in sixth grade, things changed. She got busy
with new friends, ball games, movies, and shopping.

She wasn't doing anything wrong—yet—but she had lost her
focus. She stopped reading her Bible and praying. She dropped
the most important things from her life in exchange for temporary fun. She stopped growing spiritually.

In our daily living, we must keep our purpose clearly in
mind. We are living for eternity, not for our lives here on earth.
It's easy to forget that. We get so busy—and so comfortable. We
become lazy and too concerned with our immediate happiness.
That makes it easier to slip into an ungodly lifestyle. We must

remember that like the racers in training, we haven't arrived yet either. This life is our training ground and our race.

To be sure that you finish the race with strength, do what the athletes do. Set goals for your spiritual growth, write them down, and keep track of the progress you make. Know that progress takes time, but keep at it.

Keep your eyes on Jesus, and go for the gold!

REFLECTION QUESTIONS

Do you get caught up in what's cool, what's fun? How well do you keep your focus on God and what he has to teach you?

_____

_____

_____

_____

PRAYER

Lord, I don't always remember that being a Christian
is a choice that I need to keep making. Please help me
remember that I need to focus on you *always*, not just some
of the time. I want to put you first! Thank you. Amen.

A Bounty of Blessings

"Do not be deceived: God cannot be mocked. A man reaps what he sows."

GALATIANS 6:7

Don't be misled. Remember that you can't ignore God's laws and get away with it. You always harvest what you plant. (You plant corn—you harvest corn.) You always harvest more than you plant or sow. (You plant a bushel of corn, and you reap hundreds of bushels back.) You always harvest later than you sow. (You plant corn, you wait during the growing season, and you reap during the harvest season.) The same is true of your actions—your seeds.

You always get the kind of harvest that matches your seed. A farmer plants corn expecting a harvest of corn—not carrots. Your harvest will also match the seed you sow. Galatians 6:8 says, "Whoever sows to please their flesh, from the flesh will reap destruction; whoever sows to please the Spirit, from the Spirit will reap eternal life."

So this principle works both positively and negatively. Those determined to do whatever they please, no matter what God's Word says, can count on reaping a bad harvest of problems and destruction. For those living a godly lifestyle, it is a promise of reward and blessings, and an encouragement to persist in doing what's right.

Anything you do for someone else's good is a seed you sow. It might be a smile, an encouraging word, making time to listen, praying for someone, doing a favor for your mom—it's all good seed to plant when done from an unselfish heart with unselfish motives.

Your future lies in the generous seeds you plant today.

Reflection Questions

Think about the past day or two. What do you think you've been sowing? Were you encouraging and helpful? Or were you sulking and mean-spirited?

_____

_____

_____

_____

Prayer

Lord, I don't always remember that everything I do makes a difference. I want to plant the right seeds for those around me. Please help me to rely on you and to do the right thing in everything I do. Amen.

DAY 28

PROMISE TO BE PATIENT

"Imitate those who through faith and patience inherit what has been promised."

HEBREWS 6:12

The Bible is full of promises for the believer, promises for peace, success, joy, love, friendship, rewarding work, and much more. It takes two things for these promises to come true. The first ingredient is faith: believing God's Word is true. The second ingredient is patience: keeping a positive attitude while you wait. Many believers have faith; few have patience. You need both. "After he had *patiently endured*, he obtained the promise" (Hebrews 6:15 NKJV, emphasis added).

Jillian's best friend was moving away. They'd been best friends and next-door neighbors for five years, and Jillian was brokenhearted at the news. She claimed Psalm 147:3: "[God] heals the brokenhearted and binds up their wounds." She truly believed God would do that for her, but when a week went by and she still felt sad, she decided the promise didn't work. Jillian was wrong. The promise is sure, and God's Word can be counted on. Jillian had faith—but she didn't have patience.

Patience is the ability to stay steady during the challenging storms of life. You usually have to wait what feels like a long time before you receive your promise. It's like planting a seed (your faith), then waiting for the harvest to appear. The waiting time is the testing time. Will we continue to believe God for the promise when things get tough? Will we trust that God is bringing his promises to pass even before we see the results? "Let us hold tightly without wavering to the hope we affirm, for God can be trusted to keep his promise" (Hebrews 10:23 NLT).

Are you waiting for a promise of God in your life? Then practice both faith and patience. It's a winning combination.

Reflection Questions

How's your patience level? Can you stick things out, or do you want things done right away? The next time something seems to take too long, talk to God and ask him to strengthen you.

Prayer

Lord, it's so hard to be patient. I really do want to wait for your perfect timing. Please help me stay calm and know you are taking care of everything. Thank you for all you do for me. Amen.

FOLLOWING THE PATHS OF RIGHTEOUSNESS

"Whether you turn to the right or to the left, your ears will hear a voice behind you, saying, 'This is the way; walk in it.'"

ISAIAH 30:21

God promises to lead us and guide us when we don't know what to do. As believers, we have the Holy Spirit living inside us. He is always there to help us find the right path. If we are truly listening, we'll hear that "still small voice" inside giving us sure directions.

Ashley doesn't know what to do. She just found out that her friend Merissa copied her math homework and turned it in as her own. Ashley knows cheating is wrong, but she doesn't want to make her friend mad. What's the right thing to do? Kyla can only sign up for one activity in the summer, but she loves both swimming and softball. Which one should she choose?

We all need to make decisions—big and little—many times each day. How do we know the right choices to make? The key is your relationship with God. The closer you are to him, the easier you will hear his voice and direction.

Being close to God means learning what he likes and dis-likes through reading his Word. Hearing God clearly requires that we give up what *we* want and are willing to do what *he* wants.

Hearing from God often takes time, so it calls for patience and prayer. If you're willing to do these things consistently, you'll find it much easier to hear God's voice when you need guidance.

Remember, God knows everything about your situation, even though it looks confusing to you. And he says, "I will lead the blind by ways they have not known, along unfamiliar paths I will guide them; I will turn the darkness into light before them and make the rough places smooth" (Isaiah 42:16).

When you need direction, go to God. He is a sure and trustworthy guide.

Reflection Questions

Do you have times when you just don't know what to do? Who do you turn to first? Is it God? Your mom? A friend?

_____

_____

_____

_____

Prayer

Lord, I have times when I don't know what to do. Please guide me and show me what to do. You want what is best for me, and I thank you so much for that! Amen.

LET THEM KNOW YOU BY YOUR LOVE

"If we love our brothers and sisters who are believers, it
proves that we have passed from death to life. But a person
who has no love is still dead."

I JOHN 3:14 (NLT)

If our lives have been changed by Jesus, we'll prove it by the love
we show toward others. When we fail to act in love, we are still
walking in darkness. Jesus told his closest followers, "By this
all will know that you are My disciples, if you have love for one
another" (John 13:35 NKJV).

Jenna and Samantha were at church camp. They refused to
hang out with the other three girls in their bunkhouse, secretly
believing that they were cooler than them. Although Jenna and
Samantha sang the praise songs, they weren't showing love
toward others. They walked in spiritual darkness.

The proof that you're a believer is in how you treat others.
Yes, we all get hurt and offended sometimes. We're all imperfect
human beings trying to live together. But are you truly making
an effort to love others? Do you forgive people and show them
concern and respect? When someone offends you, are you out-
wardly nice, but hold a grudge and avoid that person forever?
"Dear children, let's not merely say that we love each other; let
us show the truth by our actions" (1 John 3:18 NLT).

If we're not trying to grow and walk in loving relationship with the people around us—at home, at school, at church—we're just proving that God hasn't touched our lives. Jesus said people would know his disciples by their love for one another (see John 13:35). If people were to judge you by the love you show to others, what would they believe about you?

Grow daily in the expressions of your love toward others— and see what joy fills your heart!

Reflection Questions

When you interact with others, are you fake, or does the condition of your heart match your words? When God looks at your heart, what does he see?

_____

_____

_____

_____

Prayer

Lord, please help me to be loving, on both the outside and the inside. I want to be a great example of your love. Thank you! Amen.

DAY 31

Don't Fool Yourself

"Do not merely listen to the word, and so deceive your-
selves. Do what it says."

JAMES 1:22

It's great to read the Bible and hear it preached and pay attention
to it. But don't stop there! Practice what it says. Carry out its
directions. If you don't, you are only fooling yourself into thinking you're a follower of Christ.

When bad things happen, we often pray more and eagerly
search our Bibles for answers. That's exactly the right thing to
do, but we might not like what we find. The bully on the bus who
trips you? The Word says you are to pray for those who persecute you and pick on you, but not take revenge. How about the
classmate who makes nasty remarks or calls you mean names?
It hurts a lot. The Bible says we are to speak the truth IN LOVE
to this person, not call her names back. Don't fool yourself into
thinking that you're behaving like a Christian just by reading
the Bible. You must also do what it says.

Pray for that bully. Deal with that nasty classmate with kind
words.

Don't be someone God says this about: "I called you so often,
but you wouldn't come. I reached out to you, but you paid no
attention. You ignored my advice and rejected the correction I

offered" (Proverbs 1:24–25 NLT). Instead, be determined to put into practice what you read. You won't do it perfectly, and that's okay. But as best you can, carry out what you believe God is telling you to do in a situation.

The Word is powerful. Put it into practice, and see what marvelous changes God makes in your life.

Reflection Questions

When faced with a tough situation, do you turn to God? Do you read the Bible and do what it says?

_____

_____

_____

_____

Prayer

Lord, thank you for giving me your Word.
Help me to read it and obey. Thank you
for giving me guidance. Amen.

THE BLESSINGS OF OBEDIENCE

"If you fully obey the LORD your God and carefully follow all his commands I give you today, . . . all these blessings will come on you and accompany you."

DEUTERONOMY 28:1–2

Everybody wants to be full of peace and joy and have all their needs met. God tells you how that can happen. It's really quite simple. If you want to be blessed, be careful to follow God's commands and fully obey them. If you will do this, God's blessings of protection and abundance will attach themselves to you!

Do you want to be healthier? If you show self-control (a fruit of the Spirit) in your eating and exercise habits, you will be blessed with better health. Do you want to have the latest smartphone? Then handle your money and your job opportunities according to God's principles (like working hard and finishing what you start). Do you want the blessing of deep friendships? Then be obedient to commands like thinking of others' interests before your own.

We must be willing to do what God says to do if we want to experience what God has promised. He has given us guidelines for living a happy, blessed life, but it's up to each of us to follow those guidelines. In many, many cases, we are responsible for the outcome of our future. Although God wants to bless all of us, many of us cut off our own blessings by disobedience in some area. Jesus said, "Blessed are those who hear the word of God and keep it!" (Luke 11:28 NKJV).

Want a super-blessed life? Then dig into the Word of God and start obeying your way to blessings!

Reflection Questions

Do you have needs or wants that have not been fulfilled yet? Are they things you want, or what God wants? (Or both?)

_____

_____

_____

_____

Prayer

Lord, there are always lots of things I want, but I know that you might want different things for me. Help me to read the Bible every day and keep praying, to find out what you want me to do. Your will be done! Amen.

HONOR YOUR FRIENDSHIPS

"Our purpose is to please God, not people. He alone examines the motives of our hearts. Never once did we try to win you with flattery, as you well know. And God is our witness that we were not pretending to be your friends just to get your money!"

1 THESSALONIANS 2:4–5 (NLT)

The reason for your actions should be to please God, not people. God tests and knows the purposes hidden in your heart, the reasons for how you treat your friends. Do not try to win friends with false flattery. And don't pretend to be friends with someone because of what you can get out of it.

When someone who rarely speaks to you suddenly compliments your outfit or your science project or your hair, don't you get a little suspicious? Most of us have a good sense for false praise and flattery. Our first thought is: *Okay, what do you want from me?* Have you caught *yourself* doing the same thing with friends sometimes? Do you give honest praise? Or do you flatter someone so she'll invite you to her party or give you a ride to the game?

Paul says in this verse that personal profit was never his aim in treating his friends well: "You know we never used flattery, nor did we put on a mask to cover up greed" (1 Thessalonians 2:5).

Don't wear a mask around your friends. Don't try to hide the reasons for things you say and do. Be honest with your praise, but watch your reasons for it. Do it out of love, not to get something in return. If you're not sure of your reasons, use this as your test: Will these words and actions please God, or just people?

Please God first in your friendships—and you'll be a true friend!

Reflection Questions

Look at your friendships. Are you friends because you honestly like them or because of what they can give you? How would God see your friendships?

_____

_____

_____

_____

Prayer

Lord, I sometimes think too selfishly. Help me to
be honest with everyone I meet, including you.
Thank you for your loving care. Amen.

DAY 34

UNSHAKABLE TRUST

"They will have no fear of bad news;
their hearts are steadfast, trusting in the LORD."

PSALM 112:7

Some people have no anxiety about coming danger or receiving
bad news. Their minds and emotions are steady, firm, unwaver-
ing, and unshakable. How do they attain this wonderful state of
being? By trusting in the Lord, relying on him, putting their faith
in him, and obeying his commands.

We all receive bad news sometimes. That's part of life. It
might be fairly minor, like your friend can't go to the movies with
you after all. It might be more serious, like getting an F on your
report card. Or the bad news can be extremely painful, like the
death of a favorite grandparent or your parents' divorce. We find
it very easy to get upset at bad news, crying and screaming and
lashing out at people, or becoming severely depressed. But we're
supposed to have a calm, steadfast heart that trusts in the Lord.

A heart with unshakable faith is needed so we can stop, pray
for wisdom, and sit back and allow God to work. God will handle
those problems that we don't have the ability to control. Things
change constantly, and some of those changes will be bad. But
God never changes. His love is unchanging and everlasting.

He can (if we let him) work even bad things out for our good (Romans 8:28).

Always remember that the bad news you receive does NOT take God by surprise. He knows when it is coming, and he's ready to help you get through it, so that you come out on the other side even stronger.

Trust in God, no matter what kind of news you receive. He'll never let you down!

Reflection Questions

When you get bad news, how do you feel? What do you usually do? Do you pray to God about it?

_____

_____

_____

_____

Prayer

Lord, when bad things happen, I am not usually calm.
Please help me stay calm and have firm faith in you.
Thank you for never leaving my side. Amen.

THE TRUTH SHALL SET YOU FREE

"Caleb silenced the people before Moses and said, 'We should go up and take possession of the land, for we can certainly do it.' But the men who had gone up with him said, 'We can't attack those people; they are stronger than we are.'"

NUMBERS 13:30–31

After wandering in the wilderness for forty years, the Israelites finally arrived at the Promised Land. Twelve men were sent as spies into the land, to bring back a report. Only two men, Joshua and Caleb, had a positive report. They believed God and encouraged the people to take possession of the Promised Land. But the other ten spies were afraid, and they discouraged the people from trying. They ignored the truth of God's power, looked at the "facts" (their own small strength), and decided they couldn't conquer the cities there.

Do you ever do that? Do you spend time telling God or other people how big your problems are and how small your strength is to overcome them? Do you say, "I just can't do it" or "I can't take this anymore"? Or do you speak God's truth, which says, "I can do everything through Christ, who gives me strength" (Philippians 4:13 NLT)? When you have a fight with your best friend or your parents, do you listen to your emotions and wail, "Nobody loves me!" Or do you repeat Jesus' words from John 15:9 (NLT), which says, "I have loved you even as the Father has loved me"?

Use your mouth for the purpose God created it. Choose to believe and speak God's truth, not your fears. Don't be like the Israelite spies who stared at the "facts" and forgot about God's power. Those unbelieving men were never allowed to enter the Promised Land.

There may be some unpleasant "facts" in your life right now, but get into the Word of God. Find out God's truth on the matter. Then choose to speak it!

REFLECTION QUESTIONS

Do you ever make problems bigger than they really are? Do you ever ask God for peace about your problems?

_____

_____

_____

_____

PRAYER

Lord, I know I complain about my problems sometimes. I guess I want sympathy from other people. Please help me remember that you already know about my problems and you will get me through them. Thank you! Amen.

DAY 36

FIGHTING DISCONTENT

"Don't love money; be satisfied with what you have. For
God has said, 'I will never fail you. I will never abandon you.'"

HEBREWS 13:5 (NLT)

Keep your life free from envy, wishing you had money or things
that belong to someone else. Be content with the things you have.
You don't need to be afraid. God will provide for your needs. He
is totally dependable, and he'll never leave you in the lurch. You
can count on him!

Kelsey was content with her clothes until she visited Britney,
who had a walk-in closet full of outfits. Rosa liked the homemade
curtains and decorations in her room till she hung out in the mall
and saw the things she could have if only she had more money.
Both girls came home dissatisfied; their own clothes and rooms
suddenly seemed shabby and outdated. Instead of trusting God
to meet their needs, both girls had fallen into a big trap: envy.

Has envy over someone else's possessions ever gripped you?
You can be free if you want to regain your contentment. First,
if you always come home depressed from the mall or your rich
friend's house, then limit your time spent there. Invite friends
to your home instead, providing fun activities instead of fancy
furnishings. Also, be thankful. Thank God daily for the blessings
in your life, for the roof over your head, for your bed and clothes

and food. The more you thank God for never failing you, the more content you will grow with the things you already have.

If there's something you truly need, God will provide. In the meantime, be satisfied!

Reflection Questions

When was the last time you felt envious of someone? Does it eat at you? Ask God to help you be content with what you have.

_____

_____

_____

_____

Prayer

Lord, sometimes I feel envious of other people's things. Please take that feeling away. I want to be content with what I have. Thank you for providing all I really need. Amen.

A Friend in Times of Trouble

"Do not be afraid, for I have ransomed you.
    I have called you by name; you are mine.
When you go through deep waters,
    I will be with you.
When you go through rivers of difficulty,
    you will not drown.
When you walk through the fire of oppression,
    you will not be burned up;
    the flames will not consume you.
For I am the LORD, your God,
    the Holy One of Israel, your Savior."

ISAIAH 43:1–3 (NLT)

If you have accepted Jesus as your Savior, you don't need to be afraid anymore. God has saved and reclaimed you. Now you belong to him. Even when troubles seem too big to survive, God will walk you through them. You won't drown in your difficulty. You won't be destroyed, no matter how hard it gets sometimes.

Even when you forget to pray, God never leaves you. When you fail in your tests and trials, he never leaves you. Although you may not feel God's presence, he never leaves you. Life can sometimes hand us some very deep rivers of trouble. You may be adjusting to a new stepfamily. Your health may be in serious danger. You may have a family member fighting in the military. You may live in a city where serious crime happens daily. Is God still there, walking beside you? YES!

If you can't feel God's presence, pray. Often. The more you talk to God, the more closely you will feel him nearby. Then you will be able to say, like the apostle Paul, "The Lord stood at my side and gave me strength . . . The Lord will rescue me from every evil attack and will bring me safely to his heavenly kingdom" (2 Timothy 4:17–18).

God walks beside you daily, to encourage, protect, and comfort you. You belong to him!

Reflection Questions

Do you ever feel alone when things aren't going right? Have you talked to God about what's happening?

_____

_____

_____

_____

Prayer

Lord, you know what I'm going through. Please give me your peace and hope. I need your help to get through this. Thank you. Amen.

THE INFLUENCE OF ANGER

"Do not make friends with a hot-tempered person,
do not associate with one easily angered,
or you may learn their ways
and get yourself ensnared."

PROVERBS 22:24–25

Keep away from angry, short-tempered people. Don't make friends with them, or you will learn to be like them. This sets a snare—or a trap—for your soul.

Tamara is new at school, and two girls have been friendly to her. One girl is cynical and bullies others to get her own way. The second girl is quiet when she's upset, nursing her anger and refusing to talk to people. Which girl should she choose for a friend? Actually, neither. One is obviously a hothead, and she's easy to spot. But the girl who is easily offended, holds a grudge, and gives people the silent treatment is also an angry girl. Different personalities show anger in different ways.

Hot-tempered people can be strangely attractive. They seem to have a lot of power. No one tells them what to do. They don't put up with anything they don't like. People give in to them to keep the peace. That's what a snare is: something that looks attractive, but it's fooling you. It's like beautiful bait on a fishhook—and once you bite, you're caught. Hanging around with angry, bitter people, seeing how they handle their lives and problems, can teach you to be just like them. The Bible says these are the characteristics of a hot-tempered man: he's reckless and does foolish things (Proverbs 14:16–17), stirs up disagreements and strife (Proverbs 15:18), and commits many sins (Proverbs 29:22). Is this the kind of behavior you hope to learn? Then don't make friends with an angry, hotheaded person.

Instead, be slow to anger, and choose your friends wisely.

Reflection Questions

Are you easily offended? Do you ever shoot off your mouth without thinking? Do you know someone who does? How do you think God feels about that?

_____

_____

_____

_____

Prayer

Lord, sometimes I lose my cool and say things I don't mean. Please help me to stay calm when I get angry. I want to show others your example. Thank you! Amen.

DAY 39

FORGIVE OR BE FORGOTTEN

"If you forgive other people when they sin against you, your heavenly Father will also forgive you. But if you do not forgive others their sins, your Father will not forgive your sins."

MATTHEW 6:14–15

People hurt us or do wrong things to us, sometimes accidentally, and sometimes on purpose. Either way, we need to forgive them if we expect God to forgive us for the things we do wrong. If we refuse to forgive others, God will not forgive our sins either.

Serena got along well with everyone at school—except Timothy. He tormented her every chance he got. She had no idea why she was his target. Serena went to church, read her Bible, and prayed regularly. She forgave everyone who hurt her—except Timothy. His treatment was so mean, so unfair, that she was sure God would understand. But God doesn't make exceptions to the forgiveness rule.

We want God to forgive us for the wrongs we have done. And he will . . . unless we refuse to forgive someone else. Part of the Lord's Prayer says, "Forgive us our debts, as we forgive our debtors" (Matthew 6:12 NKJV). This means we are asking God to forgive us *in the same way* we forgive others. If we hold a grudge and refuse to forgive, God won't forgive us. But if we freely forgive, we'll be forgiven.

So start your day with a clean conscience: totally forgiven.

REFLECTION QUESTIONS

Do you need to forgive someone? Are bitter feelings coming between you and God's forgiveness?

_____

_____

_____

_____

PRAYER

Lord, if there is anyone I need to forgive, please help me to know. I want to be right with you. Please help me to forgive them and let go of past bitterness. Thank you. Amen.

GOD IS ALWAYS THERE

"I call to God,
and the LORD saves me.
Evening, morning and noon
I cry out in distress,
and he hears my voice."

PSALM 55:16–17

No matter what time it is—morning, noon, or night—God is never too busy to listen when you call on him. When you have troubles—regardless of the kind or how serious they are—God hears and answers. The Lord rescues!

When Lauren woke up and rolled over, the pain in her shoulder reminded her of her bike accident and broken collarbone. "God, I know I shouldn't complain," she whispered, "but I really hate wearing this brace! It's ugly, and I can't run now, and it hurts worse than the doctor said it would. Help me!" Did God hear her cry? Absolutely.

When Lauren lay quietly, other things came to her mind: how lucky she was not to be killed when the car hit her, how blessed she was with a mom who helped her dress, how lucky she was to have friends who carried her books, and how fortunate she was to live in a country where doctors were available to set her bones. By the time she was done praying—which is both talking *and* listening to God—Lauren felt grateful, not unlucky.

We can trust that God hears us when we cry out to him. We can trust him to handle the concerns we face each day, and to identify every worry and care that troubles us. By giving up ownership of our worries, we transfer the problem to God to solve. "Give all your worries and cares to God, for he cares about you" (1 Peter 5:7 NLT). Handing over our cares to God requires faith: we trust God will support us as he has promised.

If you need help—any time of the day or night—call on God. He's got all the time in the world to listen to you.

REFLECTION QUESTIONS

When you have troubles, do you dwell on them? Or do you count your blessings? Do you talk to God about your troubles?

_____

_____

_____

_____

PRAYER

Lord, I know things won't be perfect for me. When I am in pain or have problems, help me to come to you and give you my fears. Thank you for everything you give me daily. Amen.

DAY 41

Tested by Fire

"These trials will show that your faith is genuine. It is being tested as fire tests and purifies gold—though your faith is far more precious than mere gold."

1 PETER 1:7 (NLT)

The problems you run into are common to all believers. These difficult times test your faith, to show that it is strong. Going through tests successfully also helps to strengthen your character. It's like fire that purifies gold and brings its impurities to the surface. Your faith in God is being tested as fire tests gold—and your faith is worth far more to God than any precious metal.

Storms of life *will* come. Jesus has promised to be with us WHEN we walk through fiery trials and tests, not IF we go through tests. He's with us, alongside us, to encourage us not to faint or give up. A test in life is like a test at school: you either pass or fail. If you look at your math test, try a couple of problems, and then quit because it's too hard, you'll fail the test. Fail enough tests, and you'll have to repeat that class or grade. On the other hand, preparing yourself and trying your hardest will help you pass the test.

The same applies to the tests you'll encounter in life, whether they are friendship tests, schoolwork tests, or moral tests. If you quit when things get hard, you'll fail the test. God will forgive you; he'll pick you up and dust you off—but you'll have to repeat the test. Studying for the tests of life—reading and thinking deeply about what God's Word says to do—will help you pass your tests and come out much stronger.

Be determined to come through your tests strong and pure—more precious than gold.

REFLECTION QUESTIONS

When you have a test at school, how hard do you study? Do you think you are as well prepared for trials that life will send you?

_____

_____

_____

_____

PRAYER

Lord, I know there will be trials in my life. Please help me to be prepared for them. I want to read the Bible more and talk with you. Thank you for never leaving me. Amen.

THE PRICE OF THE PRIZE

"Everyone who competes in the games goes into strict training. They do it to get a crown that will not last, but we do it to get a crown that will last forever."

I CORINTHIANS 9:25

The Greeks had games similar to our summer Olympics. Athletes who competed were in very strict training for months beforehand. They had to develop strict self-control in their eating, drinking, rest times, and physical workouts. They did all that to win a prize that wouldn't last. The prize was a crown—not a royal crown, but a wreath or circular band made of leaves and flowers. Believers are training to win a crown that lasts forever.

Bobbi was in gymnastics. She practiced two hours a day, got up early on Saturdays for private lessons, and kept a strict diet to keep in top form. She intended to win a medal at the national competition. Lindsay read her Bible and prayed before bedtime and got up early on Sundays to make it to Sunday school. She skipped PG-13 and R-rated movies, even though she was ridiculed for it. She wanted to win a prize too. Bobbi's medal would eventually rust. Lindsay's prize would last forever.

Strict training for athletes sometimes includes muscle cramps, sports injuries, and accidents. But to win the game, sportsmen are willing to endure pain. Sadly, few Christians are willing to endure pain in order to grow in their spiritual lives. They concentrate too much on the pain and not enough on the reward that's coming. Believers can learn much from dedicated athletes. We too need to focus on the prize, a crown that will last for eternity. Your focus will determine your attitude about whatever pain or hardships you encounter.

Keep your eye on the prize!

REFLECTION QUESTIONS

Do you enjoy any sports or hobbies? How hard do you work at them? How hard do you work to improve your relationship with God?

_____

_____

_____

_____

PRAYER

Lord, I make time for some activities, but I seem to run out of time when it comes to you. Please help me to remember to use my energy for you first. I want to know more about you. Thank you. Amen.

DAY 43

A DIRECT LINE TO GOD

"When I am in distress, I call to you,
because you answer me."

PSALM 86:7

When we spot trouble—crimes, fires, car accidents—we call 911 for emergency help. We are confident when we dial 911 that the call will be answered. Help is on its way. In the same manner, you have a hotline to heaven. God's phone line is never busy, and you never get put on hold. You can talk to God anytime—day or night. And his answers are always available in his Word.

Rosa took a wrong turn on the way home, and suddenly she was biking through a creepy neighborhood she didn't recognize. She was scared! Janelle went to pay for her hamburger and discovered her purse was empty. What should she do? Anna came home from vacation to find that her best friend had a *new* best friend. Who could Anna talk to?

They all needed to call God for help. If YOU need help, try these "emergency numbers":

When you're in danger, call Psalm 91.
When God seems far away, call Psalm 139.
When you're lonely and fearful, call Psalm 23.
When you need peace and rest, call Matthew 11:28-30.

When you need courage for a task, call Joshua 1.

When you're depressed, call Psalm 27.

When you're sad or troubled, call John 14.

When you need forgiveness, call Psalm 51.

When you're worried, call Matthew 6:25-34.

We all need help sometimes. You can always pray, and you can go to God's Word. God promises to meet your needs. So give God a call!

Reflection Questions

Now that you know you can talk to God about anything, who can help you find answers in the Bible? Who can support you as you work on getting closer to God?

_____

_____

_____

_____

Prayer

Lord, thank you for the Bible and for loved ones who can help me. Thank you for always being there for me. I love you! Amen.

DAY 44

LIVING IN PEACE

"If it is possible, as far as it depends on you, live at peace with everyone."

ROMANS 12:18

Do your part to live in peace with everyone, as much as possible. If someone is acting immature, or they just irritate you, hold your tongue and keep the peace. "Depart from evil and do good; seek peace and pursue it" (Psalm 34:14 NKJV). The "evil" you need to depart from is complaining, criticizing, picking fights, and gossiping. The "good" is holding your tongue, or speaking words of encouragement. You are to seek peace and *pursue* it. It won't just fall in your lap. You have to go after peace diligently.

You are to live peacefully with people *if* it is possible, but it's not always possible. Some people simply like to fight and make trouble. Sometimes they're bored, and they find it entertaining to stir up turmoil. Avoid them. Also know this: it's not always possible to do the right thing and still get along with everyone. If a person is doing something wrong (like lying or cheating), then speak up. You are to keep the peace, but not at any price.

If Amber is shopping with Caitlin, and Amber thinks the new shoes Caitlin bought are ugly, she needs to live in peace by keeping her opinion to herself. But it's a different matter if she sees Caitlin steal from the shoe store. Yes, it will make Caitlin upset and angry if Amber confronts her, but it would be wrong for Amber to go along with it and keep quiet. Sometimes we keep silent (or keep the peace) when others do wrong so that we won't lose a friendship or lose acceptance. This is a wrong reason to live in peace.

Peace is a fruit of the Holy Spirit, and it takes time and patience to grow fruit. Do your part to live in peace with all people.

Reflection Questions

Do you like to have peace in your life? Do you think life is boring if things aren't stirred up? Who is someone you need to make peace with?

_____

_____

_____

_____

Prayer

Lord, I know I don't always promote peace around me. Please help me to be patient and peace-loving with those I'm with. Please help me to know when— and when *not*—to speak up. Thank you. Amen.

DAY 45

WHO AM I?

"You have not received a spirit that makes you fearful slaves.
Instead, you received God's Spirit when he adopted you as
his own children. Now we call him, 'Abba, Father.'"

ROMANS 8:15 (NLT)

If you've accepted Jesus as your Savior, then you've been adopted into God's family. You've been taken in as a member, with all the rights of any other son or daughter. And you have the privilege and honor to call God your Father.

Nicole sometimes felt like a big nobody. At school, people made fun of her. At home, her parents seemed to forget she existed. But Nicole knew Jesus. He'd been her Savior since she was eight years old. Because of that, Nicole knew she was somebody special.

If you don't feel special or loved or important, remember who you are in Christ:

You are Christ's friend (John 15:15).
Jesus chose you to bear good fruit for him (John 15:16).
You are a temple, or home, for God. His Spirit lives in you
    (1 Corinthians 3:16; 6:19).
You are God's workmanship (or handiwork), created in
    Christ to do his work that he planned beforehand that
    you should do (Ephesians 2:10).

You are chosen of God and dearly loved (Colossians 3:12). You are a child of God. You will resemble Christ when he returns (1 John 3:1–2).

Memorize one or more of these verses. Then, when you're in a situation that makes you feel like a nobody, speak those verses right out loud. You're a daughter of the King. You've been adopted into his royal family.

You're *very* special to God.

REFLECTION QUESTIONS

Do you ever feel ignored or unloved? What do you do when you feel unimportant? What verse will you memorize now for help later?

_____

_____

_____

_____

PRAYER

Lord, sometimes I feel like no one loves me. Please help me remember that you always love me, that I am important to you. Thank you for loving me. Amen.

Acceptance Guaranteed

"Those the Father has given me will come to me, and I will
never reject them."

JOHN 6:37 (NLT)

Jesus said he would never reject or push away anyone who
trusted in him. We just need to go to him. He knows we aren't
perfect, but he approves of us and accepts us and lives in us! No
matter who on this earth rejects you, Jesus will never reject you.

We all want the acceptance and approval of friends and family members. Rejection is one of the hardest, most painful things
we have to endure in this life. Classmates may reject us because
we look different or have little money. Family members may treat
us with scorn or disregard our wishes and opinions, almost as if
we're invisible.

The worst rejection, however, is when we reject ourselves.
We decide that because someone else doesn't like us or accept
us that there must be something wrong with us. Many of us are
very gifted and talented—in art, music, writing, singing. But we're
afraid to express ourselves because we fear the rejection of others.
What will they think of us? Will they laugh and point fingers?

Jesus accepts you just the way you are. He knew you weren't
perfect when he saved you. He knows you have weaknesses
and that you make mistakes. Even so, he will never reject you.

Nothing can ever come between you and God's love for you. "I am convinced that nothing can ever separate us from God's love. Neither death nor life, neither angels nor demons, neither our fears for today nor our worries about tomorrow—not even the powers of hell can separate us from God's love" (Romans 8:38 NLT).

Spend time with the Lord. His love will transform your life.

REFLECTION QUESTIONS

Have you ever felt rejected by someone? Did you feel like there was something wrong with you? Did you ask God to help you with those feelings?

_____

_____

_____

_____

PRAYER

Lord, when I'm rejected by someone, I feel so unworthy. I know you love me no matter what. Please help me remember that you care for me and that I'm worth a lot to you! Thank you! Amen.

HEAVENLY SANTA CLAUS?

"If you remain in me and my words remain in you, ask whatever you wish, and it will be done for you."

JOHN 15:7

Jesus himself said that if we stay joined to him, and his words continue to live in us, that we can make any request we desire, and it will be granted to us! That is one awesome promise!

Lily wanted so much to have a new jacket like her friends had. She knew that God had promised to meet all her needs, so she prayed and prayed for that new jacket. She never did get it though. And we don't always get what we pray for. Why?

It might be that you've asked for something that's not God's will for your life. People tend to concentrate on the "asking and receiving" part. But the Bible says IF you remain and abide in Jesus—and IF his words remain and stay in you—THEN you can ask what you desire and be assured of the answer. When we abide or live in him (and not just visit occasionally), we are trusting him all the time, learning from him, leaning on him, reading and studying his Word daily, and in frequent prayer about things. We are searching to know the mind of Christ.

As we do this day by day, our will is joined with his. His desires become our desires; our concerns become the same as his. More of our prayers are according to God's will, so more are answered. Very often he changes our desires to match his. We become like Jesus as we abide in him. The more we get to know him, the more fruit he produces in our lives.

Can anyone really ever have such a close relationship with Jesus? The Bible says we can—IF we are willing to take the time to get to know him. Why not try it?

REFLECTION QUESTIONS

When you pray, do you stick to the "asking for what you want" part? Do you ever ask God what he wants for you?

_____

_____

_____

_____

PRAYER

Lord, I know I ask for many things, but I don't always listen to you like I should. Please help me to listen and follow you first. I know you will give me what I really need. Thank you. Amen.

DAY 48

LEARNING TO PRAY

"One day Jesus was praying in a certain place. When he finished, one of his disciples said to him, 'Lord, teach us to pray.'"

LUKE 11:1

Jesus had the habit of prayer, of talking to his Father, praising
him and asking him for things. After one of these prayer times,
a disciple asked Jesus to teach them how to pray too.

Morgan's Sunday school teacher challenged the whole class
to pray at least ten minutes every day that week. But each time
Morgan sat down with her timer to pray, her mind went blank.
She felt guilty, but she couldn't think of anything to say. Her
mom gave her a seven-minute prayer formula, but Morgan felt
silly using it. She didn't have any success with prayer as long as
she tried to copy someone else's prayer method.

Don't try to imitate someone else's prayer life. We're all different, and our prayer lives will be different. Our life circumstances
are different too. Your grandmother who lives alone might pray
two hours every morning. You'd have to get up at 4:00 a.m. to do
that and still get to school on time.

Don't compare your prayer times to anyone else's. Instead,
talk to God. Ask him to teach you how to pray, how much to pray,
what to pray for, and how to listen for his answers.

Don't be shy about asking God for help with your prayer life.

He's willing to help you with anything. "Let us come boldly to the throne of our gracious God. There we will receive his mercy, and we will find grace to help us when we need it most" (Hebrews 4:16 NLT).

If you need help with your prayer life, be honest with God. Begin by saying, "Lord, teach me to pray."

Reflection Questions

How often do you pray? Do you know what to say, or do you find yourself stumbling along? Have you asked God for help?

_____

_____

_____

_____

Prayer

Lord, I feel so lucky to be able to talk to you whenever I need to. I'm not always sure what to say. Please help me find the words. I want a better prayer life with you. Thank you for always being there. Amen.

RESTED AND REFRESHED

"Come to me, all you who are weary and burdened, and I
will give you rest."

MATTHEW 11:28

Are you tired to the bone? Do you feel weighed down by too
much work or responsibility? Then Jesus says to come to him.
He will give you rest! He will support and steady you so you can
take a breather. He will make things easier and free you from
your duties for a while and refresh your mind and your emotions.

Annette came home from school with a headache, afraid that
she hadn't done well on her social studies test. Her legs hurt
from running a mile in gym class. She fixed her little brother a
snack and was ready to collapse when the phone rang. "I'll be
late tonight, honey," her mom said. "Can you make spaghetti and
have it ready by six?" Annette hung up and leaned against the
table. She felt overburdened.

Some days we feel so overworked, overtired, and overburdened that we can't take it anymore. Then what should we do?
Jesus said to come to him, but how do we do that? We can come
in prayer, being honest with him about how exhausted we are.
That can be physical tiredness, but it can also be mental or emotional exhaustion. Our tired emotions might be overworked from
dealing with fights or angry people or some upsetting event.

Our minds might be exhausted from too much mental work like studying or trying to figure out what to do about a problem. From ALL these things, Jesus wants to give you rest.

Are you overtired? Then take five or ten minutes, close your eyes, and breathe deeply. Ask Jesus to refresh your mind, body, and emotions. Soak it up. Take your time. Ahhhh . . .

REFLECTION QUESTIONS

Have you felt really tired this past week? Why do you think you were so worn down? Did you know you can rest in Jesus?

_____

_____

_____

_____

PRAYER

Lord, I'm so tired. My body and mind need to be refreshed. Please give me rest. Please help me stay rested by staying close to you. Thank you. Amen.

THREE EASY STEPS TOWARD A BETTER YOU

"Jesus said to the people who believed in him, 'You are truly my disciples if you remain faithful to my teachings. And you will know the truth, and the truth will set you free.'"

JOHN 8:31–32 (NLT)

Do you feel trapped? Do you need freedom from something? If you're a believer, obey Jesus' teachings. Then you will learn the truth deep down where it counts—and it's this truth that will set you free.

Dawn made friends easily, but she lost them fast. Dawn often would explode in anger over minor things. She didn't give her friends a chance to explain why they were late or what they meant by something they said. Dawn was tired of losing friends, but she felt trapped by her short temper.

You can be trapped by depression, fear, a bad temper, gossip, the list goes on. The answer is the same, no matter what you need freedom from: learn the truth, obey, and be set free. The behavior comes *before* the feeling of freedom.

Do you have a temper that ruins relationships? Be set free!

Get the truth from God's Word: "Be quick to listen, slow to speak, and slow to get angry" (James 1:19 NLT).

Believe the truth: No matter how strong your feelings are, believe the truth. Your feelings may scream, "He makes me so mad! I can't stop the words from coming out!" Your feelings are not the truth. God's Word is the truth. And it says that you CAN be slow to get angry.

Take action: Change the behavior. First, pray for help. Then work on specific actions. (Count to ten before speaking, or leave the room. Ask questions to get all the facts.)

Feel the freedom! Strong feelings can be slow to change. But whatever you need freedom from, the steps are the same. Today, search God's Word and find the truth that will set you free.

Reflection Questions

Do you feel trapped by something? What have you tried to do about it?

_____

_____

_____

_____

Prayer

Lord, I've been feeling trapped lately. I want to be free, but I need your help. With you by my side, I will conquer this! Thank you. Amen.

REACHING GOALS: GET A CLEAR PICTURE

"David asked the soldiers standing nearby, 'What will a man get for killing this Philistine and ending his defiance of Israel? Who is this pagan Philistine anyway, that he is allowed to defy the armies of the living God?' And these men gave David the same reply. They said, 'Yes, that is the reward for killing him.'"

I SAMUEL 17:26–27 (NLT)

A giant, Goliath, was making fun of the Israelite army. David, a shepherd boy, heard that the king had offered a reward for killing the giant (including marriage to one of the king's daughters). David checked with the soldiers to see if that was true. He also asked them why the giant was allowed to challenge and resist the Israelite army, the army of the living God.

David's goal was to do what none of the soldiers had been able to do: face the giant, Goliath, and kill him for the king. But David didn't immediately run to attack Goliath. He talked to the soldiers, he learned what Goliath had been doing to them for forty days, and he learned what reward had been offered. He took time to get a clear picture of the situation.

Do you get an idea for something you'd like to do, and then rush into it without thinking or talking to others (especially God) about it? Maybe you want to win a race at a track meet. Should you immediately start running five miles every morning before school? Or should you get a clear picture first of what's needed? What will it take to make the track team? What kind of running shoes do you need to avoid injury?

Ask questions of those in charge, and get a clear picture first. Then you'll be on your way to reaching your goal!

REFLECTION QUESTIONS

When you want to do something, do you plan it out? Or do you rush into it without thinking? Do you ask God about it?

_____

_____

_____

_____

PRAYER

Lord, I have lots of ideas about how to live my life. Please help me to ask you first for guidance. I want to do what you want me to do. Thank you. Amen.

Reaching Goals: Feel the Desire

"David said to Saul, 'Let no one lose heart on account of this
Philistine; your servant will go and fight him.'"

I SAMUEL 17:32

You can feel David's passion and enthusiasm as he declares to
King Saul that he, David, will go and fight the giant insulting
Philistine. David encourages the soldiers not to lose heart (or
have their hearts and courage fail them). He's excited to meet
that challenge!

Sometimes we can get excited to face challenges too. Sara
says to Janet, "I can't wait to start the summer reading program!
I'm going to read more than fifty books and win that new e-book
reader! Want to do the reading challenge with me?" Janet says,
"Sure, I guess . . . I don't have anything better to do." Which girl
has the passionate desire to reach a goal? Who will probably be
the only one to succeed?

David's passion to fight wasn't for himself, but to strike down
the giant who mocked God and God's promises. Like David when
he faced Goliath, you also need to feel passionate about your
goals. You need to feel excited about them, with enough enthusiasm to carry you through to the finish line. Half-hearted feelings
and ho-hum attitudes won't be enough.

David also made a decision: "I will go and fight him." Being excited about doing something won't help unless you make a decision to accomplish it. Sara could get all excited ("I want to win that reader!"), but without a plan ("I will read fifty books. I'm going to the library now"), Sara would never meet her goal.

Don't lose heart! To reach your goals, you have to keep your enthusiasm and excitement alive.

Reflection Questions

When you have something you want to do, are you excited? Do you stay excited, or do you get bored and go on to something else?

_____

_____

_____

_____

Prayer

Lord, there are many things I want to do. Please help me to pray first, then plan. I want to stay excited for the plans you have for me! Thank you! Amen.

REACHING GOALS: BE CONFIDENT!

"David replied to the Philistine, "You come to me with sword,
spear, and javelin, but I come to you in the name of the LORD
of Heaven's Armies—the God of the armies of Israel, whom
you have defied. Today the LORD will conquer you.'"

I SAMUEL 17:45–46 (NLT)

When David faced Goliath, he did it with confidence. Goliath
might have had swords and weapons of war, but David had the
living God on his side. He proclaimed without any doubt that
the Lord would defeat Goliath. David was sure of God's power
working through him to succeed in his goal.

David spoke about the past victories God had given him.
Remembering how God had delivered him from attacking lions
and bears gave him confidence that God would deliver him from
Goliath too.

What goals do *you* have? Do you want to learn how to ice
skate? Do you wish you could speak Spanish? Maybe you'd like
to learn to dive or swim better. Whatever your goal, if you've
prayed about it and are sure it's something God can approve,
then be positive. Have confidence that you can achieve it.

Declare, "I know I can do this." Repeat, "I can do all things
through Christ who strengthens me" (Philippians 4:13 NKJV)
when you run into difficulties as you work toward your goals. If

you fall, get up and quote Philippians 4:13. Do it when you belly flop your first ten dives. Say it when you have tried (and failed) to learn your Spanish ABC's.

You will also need confidence when other people question you. ("Are you SURE you want to try to dive?") Some will try to discourage you. ("You'll *never* learn to speak Spanish!") David faced this when King Saul doubted his ability and wanted to dress him in better armor for the fight. David's confidence helped him fight in his own way.

Don't be wishy-washy, and don't listen to the naysayers. Reach for your goals with confidence!

Reflection Questions

Do you have confidence that your goals are from God? If not, have you asked God for confidence in what you do?

_____

_____

_____

_____

Prayer

Lord, sometimes I don't feel confident. Please help me to remember that my confidence needs to be in you instead. Thank you for giving me the strength I need. Amen.

REACHING GOALS: TAKE ACTION!

"He took his staff in his hand, chose five smooth stones
from the stream, put them in the pouch of his shepherd's
bag and, with his sling in his hand, approached the Philistine."

I SAMUEL 17:40

David didn't have any fancy, high-tech weapons, but he had a
plan. He took his shepherd's staff (a long, thick stick) and went to
the stream. There, he found five smooth stones, which he placed
in his large shepherd's bag. With his sling (a weapon used to hurl
the stones), David walked up to the giant, Goliath.

To meet your goals, you will also need to take some action
steps. If you want to learn to swim, those steps might include
buying a swimsuit, signing up for classes at the Y, and research-
ing swimming techniques. If you want to learn to paint with
watercolors, you may need to study how-to books, buy paints
and an easel, take a beginner's painting class at school, or visit
an artist's studio.

It's great to have a clear idea of what your goal is, lots of
desire to accomplish it, and tons of confidence. But unless you
take some clear steps of action, your goal will never come to
pass. David wasn't just confident. He (1) grabbed his staff,
(2) went to the stream, (3) found five stones to put in his bag,
(4) took his sling, and (5) ran up to Goliath. If you want to reach

goals—whatever they might be—you'll need to take action steps too. Enthusiasm won't take you very far. It's like a car without gas—nice, but not going anywhere.

Map out a clear plan of action, then take your first step!

Reflection Questions

Think of something you want to do. Have you made any plans on how to make it happen? Have you set deadlines for your goal?

_____

_____

_____

_____

Prayer

Lord, I really want these goals to happen. Help me to make a plan to get them done. Thank you for your support that never ends. Amen.

REACHING GOALS: MAKE A DEADLINE

"As the Philistine moved closer to attack him, David ran quickly toward the battle line to meet him."

I SAMUEL 17:48

The giant, Goliath, boldly moved closer to David to attack and kill him. David didn't run away, or call for help, or change his mind about his "sling and stone" plan. Instead, he knew that the time had come to take action. So he ran quickly to meet the Philistine, Goliath, at the battle line.

David didn't just have confidence and an action plan. He "ran quickly toward the battle line" when Goliath moved closer. He didn't say, "Well, someday soon I should do something about that giant." No, he gave himself a deadline. Goliath had already been mocking and jeering the Israelite army for forty days. David decided it was time to act *now*—not someday when he felt more like it.

You need deadlines too. If your goal is to learn watercolor painting, put deadlines for your action steps on the calendar. Sign up for those art classes; put the date of the first class on your calendar. Call that local artist, set up a time to visit his studio, and put that date on your calendar. Decide that you're going to have all your supplies gathered by the end of the month, and write that on your calendar.

If you're vague about when you want to meet your goals, they won't happen. Saying that "someday" you're going to volunteer to help in the church nursery, or "any day now" you plan to learn to play guitar isn't enough. Instead, write down the date you expect to achieve your goal. And put down time limits for each individual step too. (It's fine if it takes you longer than you think it will.) Having a deadline will motivate you to get started *now*.

Do you have a goal that excites you? Then write down a deadline for meeting it on your calendar. You're well on your way now!

REFLECTION QUESTIONS

Do you have projects you've started but haven't finished? Would giving yourself a deadline help?

_____

_____

_____

_____

PRAYER

Lord, I have good intentions, but I don't always finish what I start. Help me stay focused and finish my projects. Thank you for your loving care. Amen.

REACHING GOALS: GET SUPPORT

"Two are better than one,
   because they have a good return for their labor:
If either of them falls down,
   one can help the other up."

ECCLESIASTES 4:9–10

Some goals, especially small ones that can be done today or very soon, you can do alone. But large goals are easier to reach if you get help and support from others. Two working together are better than each person working alone. When someone helps or assists you, their efforts will be joined with yours for an even better yield or outcome.

Suppose your goal is to train your singing voice so you can sing solos someday. You can work alone, but how much better to ask for the support and help of your family, your music teacher, or your youth leader. Support from your parents might include private voice lessons. Your music teacher might give you extra practice time after school. Your youth leader might find opportunities for you to sing.

Way back in Genesis 2:18, God said it wasn't good for us to be alone. He knows we do better with help, so don't be ashamed to ask for support. Even Jesus sent his disciples out two by two when it was time for them to minister (Mark 6:7). You'll be able to reach your goals much easier (and have encouragement on the days you want to quit) if you enlist help from others.

Your ultimate help and support, of course, comes from God. He's available 24/7, while people aren't. If this is a God-given, God-approved goal, he also has the power to see that you're in the right place at the right time.

Look for help in reaching your goals, and be sure to help *others* reach theirs!

Reflection Questions

Is there something you are working toward right now? Who can help you achieve your goal? Someone at home, school, or church?

_____

_____

_____

_____

Prayer

Lord, I thank you for giving me such big dreams.
Please help me find the right people to help me.
Thank you for your love and support. Amen.

REACHING GOALS: BE PERSISTENT

"Let us not become weary in doing good, for at the proper time we will reap a harvest if we do not give up."

GALATIANS 6:9

When we start something new, we feel energetic. But on the way to meeting our goal, we will need to be persistent. Don't get tired of doing the necessary things to meet your goal, even if it takes more time than you planned. At the right and proper time, you *will* meet that goal, but only if you don't give up.

If your goal is to join the track team, you may start out with great enthusiasm. You lift weights three times a week, you jog in the morning before school, and you eat protein snacks. Several weeks into your program, though, you may find yourself bored, or tired of the routine, or just sick of eating chicken when you'd rather have french fries. If you give up at this point, you won't reach your goal. However, if you pray for help and focus again on your end result, you will get past this temptation to quit.

When you're on your way to meeting your goals, be careful not to get distracted by things that catch your attention. Being distracted can make you give up on your goal almost without realizing it. It's so easy to do! Remember when Jesus visited the home of Mary and Martha? Imagine having the Lord come to your home to talk! "But Martha was distracted by all the preparations that had to be made" (Luke 10:40). She was paying so much attention to the housework and cooking that she didn't focus on the important thing: Jesus had come to see her! So focus on the main goal. And when you're tempted to quit, keep on keepin' on!

REFLECTION QUESTIONS

When there is something you really want, do you stick to it through thick and thin? Or do all kinds of things sidetrack you?

_____

_____

_____

_____

PRAYER

Lord, this dream I have is lot of work. Help me to stay focused: on you, and on what I want to do. Please help me stay free of distractions. Thank you! Amen.

REACHING GOALS:
MANAGE YOUR EMOTIONS

"You are still worldly [controlled by ordinary impulses, the sinful capacity]. For as long as there is jealousy and strife and discord among you, are you not unspiritual, and are you not walking like ordinary men [unchanged by faith]?"

I CORINTHIANS 3:3 (AMP)

When you give in and are guided by your emotions, or those "ordinary impulses," all kinds of trouble results. It's human nature to get angry, but anger can lead to arguments, jealousy, and bitterness. If you are a follower of Christ, this should not be your behavior.

When you first announce to your friends or family that you're attempting a certain goal, you may get very unspiritual reactions. Some may express mild doubt that eats at your self-confidence. ("Are you *sure* you want to try learning Spanish?") Others will be openly negative. ("I don't think you have a chance of making the team.") Still others—jealous of your dream—can be downright nasty. ("Are you crazy? You're nuts to think you can ever sing in public.") Discouraging put-downs like this can make you angry, or discourage you to the point of wanting to quit.

It's sad, but true, that not all people will applaud your goals and dreams. People with low self-esteem—people who don't feel good about themselves—try to make themselves feel better by pulling you down. Don't listen to their discouraging comments! Remember: "I can do all things through Christ who strengthens me" (Philippians 4:13 NKJV). Control your emotional reactions to these negative comments. Pray and don't say anything until you're calm. Don't defend yourself. Simply say, "I'm sorry you feel that way," and change the subject.

Then be doubly determined to lean on God to see you through to victory!

Reflection Questions

Who do you usually go to for advice and help? Do these people come through for you, or do their remarks upset you and drag you down? Who can you turn to and count on for support?

_____

_____

_____

_____

Prayer

Lord, you know I have dreams. Not everyone thinks I can make it. Please help me to stay focused on you and what you want me to do. Thank you for being with me through the good and the bad. Amen.

REACHING GOALS: TAKE COURAGE

"As the Philistine moved closer to attack him, David ran quickly toward the battle line to meet him. Reaching into his bag and taking out a stone, he slung it and struck the Philistine on the forehead."

I SAMUEL 17:48–49

After talking and planning and preparing, David went up against the giant, Goliath, all alone. The giant was covered in his armor, while David had a rock for a weapon. He took courage, slung a rock at the giant, and met his goal. Goliath fell down dead, and Israel's army was saved.

When you are trying to achieve your goals, it's good to have the support and encouragement of others. But at some point, after all the planning and practicing, you have to take action all alone. You stand at the microphone and sing that solo—alone. You run that race—alone. You paint that picture, or write that story, or ride that horse, or get on that bike—alone. This takes courage. Without it, you won't meet your goal, even if you've faithfully followed every step until now.

Fear is a normal feeling at this point, but it's what you do with this feeling that counts. You can act like King Saul and his army when they were faced with Goliath's threats. "When Saul and the Israelites heard this, they were terrified and deeply shaken" (1 Samuel 17:11 NLT). For forty days, Saul and his men let their fear of being defeated keep them from facing Goliath. No doubt David, as a young shepherd boy, was afraid as he faced the giant. But David didn't focus on his fear and let it paralyze him. Instead, he took courage from the living God and "ran quickly toward the battle line" to meet Goliath.

When you need courage to take action, pray first. Then move ahead and reach that goal!

Reflection Questions

Are you getting close to reaching a goal or dream? How much of a hold does fear have on you? Do you feel ready to finish?

Prayer

Lord, thank you for all your love and support as
I have worked toward my goal. Please give me
the courage to finish it! I love you. Amen.

DAY 60

REACHING GOALS: LEAN ON GOD

"The battle is the LORD's."

1 SAMUEL 17:47

Just before the battle with Goliath in 1 Samuel 17, David announced to one and all that he expected God to win this battle for him: "The LORD will . . . rescue me" (v. 37), "This day the LORD will deliver [Goliath] into my hands" (v. 46), and "The LORD saves" (v. 47). David was well aware that in his own strength, he was no match at all for Goliath. Yes, David had to step up to the battle line himself, but he also depended on God to save him, "for the battle is the LORD's" (v. 47).

Because of different personalities, most believers go to extremes. Sarah prays, then sits back and says she's "just trusting the Lord" to give her good grades. (No, she's not. She's being lazy when she should be studying.) Wendy works hard from dawn to dusk, rarely prays, and believes she will succeed someday in the music field based on her own talent. (No, she won't. She's arrogant and thinks she doesn't need God's help for anything.) Be careful that you don't fall into error either way.

Successfully reaching your goals depends on two things that might, at first, seem like opposites. You need to do the work necessary to reach your goals, praying each step of the way. But you also need to understand that it is God who will give you the power to succeed. You must be prepared, but it is God who saves and provides. "The horse is prepared for the day of battle, but deliverance is of the LORD" (Proverbs 21:31 NKJV). To reach your goals, find the balance. You can't sit idle, expecting God to do the work for you. But you won't succeed in God's plans for your life if you trust in yourself, thinking you're so clever or so smart you don't need God's help.

Make a plan, be persistent, and be confident. Then, leaning on God, take action—for the battle is the Lord's.

REFLECTION QUESTIONS

How often do you pray for God's guidance? Do you sit back and wait, or do you work and prepare?

_____

_____

_____

_____

PRAYER

Lord, I believe my goals come from you. Help me to be prepared to accomplish them. Thank you for your support that never ends. Amen.

CONFIDENCE IN ME?

"[Be] confident of this very thing, that He who has begun a good work in you will complete it until the day of Jesus Christ."

PHILIPPIANS 1:6 (NKJV)

Be very sure—be confident—that God lives in you. He is working in you to mature you, and he will keep working until you're finally finished—complete and perfect.

Heather was a believer, but she didn't feel confident. She tried to ignore the girls in band who laughed when her clarinet squeaked. She pretended not to mind when the gym teacher yelled at her to pick up the pace. She turned away from her brother when he called her "Tubby." But when Heather fell into bed that night, it all came rushing back. She felt untalented, slow, and fat.

She was, in fact, NONE of those things. But the opinions of others can sometimes beat down our self-confidence.

You are a child of God. He lives in you and is working in you. You can be confident of that! To feel better about yourself, be sure to do the following things:

Never speak negatively about yourself.
Think and speak positive things about yourself.
Never compare yourself with others.

Find something you like to do—something you're good at—
and practice it over and over.
Stay close to God, your true source of confidence.

God knows that you are more precious than gold, and he is living and working in you every minute of every day. You can be confident of that!

Reflection Questions

Do you ever feel like your confidence is missing? Do you realize how much God loves you? What is one thing you can do to feel more confident today?

_____

_____

_____

_____

Prayer

Lord, when things don't go right, I can feel down
really easily. Please help me to remember that
all I need is you. Thank you for your confidence
in me that never ends. I love you! Amen.

ON TO VICTORY!

"In all these things we are more than conquerors through him who loved us."

ROMANS 8:37

No matter what kind of trouble or challenge you face right now, overwhelming victory is yours through Christ. Not just enough victory to survive or get by. No! A *super*-strong victory, through Jesus, who loves and lives in you.

The key to having victory in our lives—instead of becoming victims of others or bad circumstances—is Jesus. It is only through him that success is ours. As you lean on him and trust him to give you whatever you need, you will learn by experience that you CAN do all things through Christ, who gives you the strength (Philippians 4:13).

What kind of hard situation are you facing? Has someone in your family discovered they have a serious disease? Has your dad changed jobs, forcing you to move across the country? Did your nutritional habits change over the summer, and now you don't want to face your classmates? Do you live in a dangerous neighborhood? No matter what you face, you are *still* more than a conqueror.

God is all-powerful—more than enough for any trouble or circumstance—and his Spirit lives in us. "I will ask the Father, and He will give you another Helper, that He may be with you forever" (John 14:16 NASB). The Holy Spirit in us is our helper. As you spend time with God and talk to him and share your fears, you'll draw strength from him. Instead of focusing on your problems, keep your attention on Jesus, the problem solver.

Then be ready for a sweeping victory!

REFLECTION QUESTIONS

Are you going through a tough situation right now? Or dealing with something from the past? Did you handle it alone? How could you handle it better with God's help?

_____

_____

_____

_____

PRAYER

Lord, there are things I'm really worried about right now. I don't know what to do, but I know you will get me through this. Please help me to stay calm and trust in you. Thank you for always being there for me. Amen.

GOD KNOWS YOU INSIDE OUT

"Cultivate inner beauty, the gentle, gracious kind that God delights in."

I PETER 3:4 (MSG)

Nurture the growth of inner qualities like kindness and tenderness. Be soft and mild, with a generous spirit, not harsh or stern or severe. This is what God delights in.

Brittany dressed in the latest fashions, got expensive haircuts, and had a sharp, clever remark for everyone. It really irritated her that her neighbor, Beth, had more friends than she did. Brittany's own sister had the nerve to say she wished Brittany was more like Beth! But why? Brittany had no idea.

It's all about beauty. We have an outer life that everyone can see. But we have an inner life too, which God sees. Our reputation with God is based on our heart, our inner life. We tend to give most of our attention to our outer life, and very little to our inner life. But God doesn't watch just our actions. He examines the attitudes, motives, and desires of our heart. All these things are important to him—and to others.

The inner person is who we *really* are. People will know you're being fake when your outer behavior (acting sweet and nice) doesn't match your attitude (resentful or superior). And you will feel like a fake when you do one thing while feeling something different. True inner beauty will also be seen (and appreciated!) on the outside.

Reflection Questions

Does the way you act match how you feel on the inside? Would you be embarrassed if others could see the real you?

_____

_____

_____

_____

Prayer

Lord, my heart doesn't always match what I say and do. I want to be kind and gentle like you are. Thank you for helping me get rid of the bad attitudes in my heart. Amen.

BATTLING BEWILDERMENT

"Trust in the LORD with all your heart;
do not depend on your own understanding."

PROVERBS 3:5 (NLT)

Life can be confusing. Sometimes we just don't know what to do. Learn to lean on, trust in, and be confident in the Lord. Trust him with all your heart and mind. Don't depend on figuring things out yourself.

Do you ever wonder what God is doing in your life? You've prayed about the things that worry you, or the situations causing you distress, but nothing seems to be happening. You still can't get along with your stepsister. Your grades in math are slipping, no matter how hard you pray and study. Do you feel like God isn't listening, that you have to figure things out on your own? That kind of thinking—depending on your own mind—will only make you confused, anxious, and afraid.

As believers, we have the privilege of staying peaceful in the middle of trying times. We can trust in God even when we don't understand what has already happened, or what is going to happen in the future. We can "Rest in the LORD, and wait patiently for Him" (Psalm 37:7 NKJV).

Sometimes tragedies strike. A family member ends up in

the hospital. A tornado flattens our house. Our parents get divorced. We are shocked and bewildered. What do we do now? Remember: *nothing* that has happened took God by surprise. He knew it was coming, he has a plan, and he'll take care of you. You don't have to figure everything out! "Trust in Him at all times, you people; Pour out your heart before Him; God is a refuge for us" (Psalm 62:8 NKJV).

Learn to trust God and lean on him at all times. Trade your confusion for his peace.

REFLECTION QUESTIONS

Do you ever feel confused when making a big decision? Do you worry over it or ask God about it?

_____

_____

_____

_____

PRAYER

Lord, there's something I'm really concerned about. I don't know what to do. Please guide me and show me the way to go. Thank you for always being with me. Amen.

Crafting a Content Heart

"I have learned to be content whatever the circumstances."

PHILIPPIANS 4:11

Learn to be satisfied with how things are, no matter what is happening in your life. Whether you have too little, just enough, or more than enough, be stable and content with what God has given you.

Amber found it easier to be content with her life when her dad still had his high-paying job. When he was laid off and money became tight, Amber's spirit grew discontent. Over several months, though, Amber learned to appreciate the things she did have. She learned to enjoy movies and popcorn at home with her family instead of going out. In fact, she had to admit that she enjoyed her family a lot more now that her dad was home in the evenings.

No matter what is happening, we are to tell God what we need. While waiting for the answer to arrive, focus on all the times God has helped you in the past. "Don't worry about anything; instead, pray about everything. Tell God what you need, and thank him for all he has done" (Philippians 4:6 NLT).

If you have asked God for something that is going to be good for you, he will give you what you asked for. But rest in the knowledge that if it's not right, God will do something far better than you asked for. Trust him completely to handle the situation. "Do not throw away this confident trust in the Lord. Remember the great reward it brings you! Patient endurance is what you need now, so that you will continue to do God's will. Then you will receive all that he has promised" (Hebrews 10:35-36 NLT).

A contented heart—free from anxieties and worries—is a priceless possession. Trust God, and learn to be content.

REFLECTION QUESTIONS

Do you generally feel content? Do you worry about how much you do or don't have? Have you asked God to give you a grateful heart?

_____

_____

_____

_____

PRAYER

Lord, I tend to think a lot about what I want but don't have. Please help me to be content with what I have. I know you will give me everything I need. Thank you. Amen.

SAVED BY THE HOLY SPIRIT

"When he, the Spirit of truth, comes, he will guide you into
all the truth."

JOHN 16:13

One of the jobs of the Holy Spirit is to help us in making decisions or choosing the right path. The Holy Spirit wants to guide you. When you ask others for advice, they give you conflicting opinions. The Holy Spirit, however, knows the whole truth about the situation—all sides of it—and wants to help you make the *best* decision.

What do you need help with? Which summer school class to take? Dealing with a stressed-out parent? Solving a money problem? The Holy Spirit will guide you.

No one learns to hear from the Holy Spirit overnight. It takes time—and learning from your mistakes. But the following things can help you tune up your hearing:

Have regular prayer time with God. Don't just talk to him.
Sit and listen too.
Be careful what you feed your mind. If you watch ungodly
movies it will be harder to tune in to the Holy Spirit's
frequency.
Be willing to do God's will, even if it's not what you want.
Realize you will probably receive guidance one step at
a time, rather than a detailed plan. As you take each
obedient step, God will reveal the next step.

Have an attitude of gratitude.

Feed your mind on God's Word.

Don't do anything unless you have peace in your heart about it. Pay attention to the little warning signs that the Holy Spirit sends your way. Stop and wait until you have peace.

Get ready for an exciting adventure as the Holy Spirit guides you!

REFLECTION QUESTIONS

Do you want help with decisions but aren't sure where to turn? Do you ask God for help but aren't sure he's answering? You can trust that he hears and cares.

_____

_____

_____

_____

PRAYER

Lord, sometimes I need help, and I'm confused. I know you have the answers, if I will just listen. Please help me to be patient and wait for your answer. You are always right! Thank you. Amen.

DAY 67

I'm So Angry I Could Pray!

"Whoever is patient has great understanding,
but one who is quick-tempered displays folly."

PROVERBS 14:29

A person who controls her anger can make good judgments. She knows the best course of action in trying times. Someone with a quick temper will make stupid, costly mistakes. Which girl do you want to be? Whose life will be happier?

Wouldn't you like to have patience when bad things happen, or when you need help with something? Maybe you got ignored and sat on the bench the whole soccer game. Or your sister swiped your favorite shirt and ruined it. What's the best way to handle each situation? Giving in to your anger is NOT the best way. You'll just create even bigger problems.

It's hard to know how to deal with difficult people or circumstances if you have a quick temper. It requires patience to hear from God about what to do. An easily angered person shoots off her mouth and takes impulsive—often destructive—actions without thinking. You do a lot of damage that way. "A quick-tempered man acts foolishly, and a man of wicked intentions is hated" (Proverbs 14:17 NKJV). Only if you're patient will you be able to get God's guidance about how to handle something wisely.

Feeling anger is not wrong, but expressing that anger quickly can backfire. A big step toward controlling anger is to be slow in expressing it. Stop! Think! Pray! Tell God how angry you are—and why—and ask him for direction about what to do. Then calm down and listen. Don't do ANYTHING until you're sure what God and his Word say to do. Otherwise you may act foolishly, and your rash behavior will cause even more problems than you had before.

Endure trying circumstances with an even temper; take time to hear from God, and you'll act wisely.

REFLECTION QUESTIONS

How often do you say something in anger without thinking? Is it hard for you to stay calm and say nothing?

_____

_____

_____

_____

PRAYER

Lord, I know I sometimes don't control my anger very well.
Please help me to stay calm and to ask you for guidance.
I want to act the way you would act. Thank you. Amen.

DAY 68

LIVING THE GOOD LIFE

"The thief comes only to steal and kill and destroy; I have come that they may have life, and have it to the full."

JOHN 10:10

Satan (the thief) is interested only in himself. He wants to steal (our health, our work, our peace) and to kill (our joy, our bodies) and to destroy (our families and friendships). Jesus came for the opposite reason: to give us an abundant, joy-filled life—a life overflowing with blessings.

Life has a beginning, a middle, and an end. Your grandparents may be near the end of their lives, while you are nearer the beginning. All of life is meant to be enjoyed. Although Satan wants to ruin things for you, God wants you to enjoy the journey of your life.

Like the route for any journey or trip, life is always changing. It will be hard to enjoy your life until you understand that. Relationships are always changing—either growing or dying. Your body is growing at a rapid rate. (Just look at your baby pictures to see how you've changed!) Your schoolwork changes from year to year, getting harder. But since you've learned more, you can handle it. Sometimes God takes us through tough times because there are things we need to learn so we can more fully enjoy our lives later. No matter how good your life is right now (or how hard), it will pass. Then you'll be in a new phase to enjoy.

This time next year you'll be very different in some ways. Just don't struggle so hard trying to get to the next place that you fail to enjoy where you are right now. It's good to have goals (earning that grade, learning that ballet step, making a new friend). But remember that Jesus died so you would have a joyful, abundant life TODAY too.

Make a choice to enjoy your life to the full!

REFLECTION QUESTIONS

Are you enjoying your life as it is today, or are you wishing for things that will happen in the future? What things are you enjoying *today*?

_____

_____

_____

_____

PRAYER

Lord, I look forward to a lot of things in my life.
Help me to enjoy today and what is happening now.
Thank you for your work in my life today. Amen.

A Hope-Full Existence

"We are hard pressed on every side, but not crushed; perplexed, but not in despair; persecuted, but not abandoned; struck down, but not destroyed."

2 CORINTHIANS 4:8–9

Life can be very hard sometimes, but if you belong to Christ, you always have a sure hope. You may feel pressured, but you won't be broken. Situations may leave you bewildered and confused, but never without hope. You may be suffering, but you are never deserted or forgotten. You may feel struck down temporarily, but you will never be ruined.

Some years are easy, and some years you face fiery trials. They might come in the form of your dad being laid off from his job, or your mom needing surgery, or your house burning down. Do you ever feel confused by the suffering and trials you experience? It's normal to wonder why it has to be that way and how it's all going to work out.

Just don't be fooled into thinking you'll be destroyed by it. You always have hope because Jesus lives in you! This isn't the kind of hope you find in the world, like "I hope I get invited to that party," or "I hope it doesn't rain today." That kind of hope is flimsy wishful thinking. The kind of hope *you* have is rock solid. "May the God of hope fill you with all joy and peace as you trust in him, so that you may overflow with hope by the power of the Holy Spirit" (Romans 15:13). He's the God of hope! That's why you never have to worry, no matter what you're going through at this moment.

If you're in the middle of a heavy trial right now, talk to God frequently. Draw on his courage and hope. Then you can also say, "Yet in all these things we are more than conquerors through Him who loved us" (Romans 8:37 NKJV).

Reflection Questions

Are you going through any trials right now? Do you worry that God doesn't care, or do you talk to God about your problems?

_____

_____

_____

_____

Prayer

Lord, I have a rough time to get through. Help me to rely on you, knowing that I always have hope in you. Thank you for your everlasting love. Amen.

DAY 70

Divided, You Will Fall

"Out of the same mouth come praise and cursing. My brothers and sisters, this should not be."

JAMES 3:10

In James' letter, he described men who were praising God, yet cursing people (who are made in God's image). Thanksgiving and swearing gushed out of the same mouth. Surely, this is not good or suitable behavior for followers of Christ!

Have you ever been guilty of sitting in church, singing praise and worship songs, then going home and using your mouth to gossip with your friends in the afternoon? Gossiping, judging, and criticizing others are disgusting habits to God. He doesn't want us to praise him, then turn around and pick apart the people he created.

This "forked tongue" tends to happen for one of two reasons: we either think too much of ourselves (pride), or we think too little of ourselves (low self-esteem). If we're puffed up with pride, we'll look down on anyone who looks or acts differently from the way we act. (After all, if we're *right*, they must be wrong!) If we have low self-esteem, we may use our critical attitude toward others to make ourselves feel better than they are.

Even if someone criticizes you first, don't stoop to their level. Instead, "Bless those who persecute you; bless and do not curse" (Romans 12:14). Nobody on earth is perfect; not us, and not others. Once we acknowledge that, we'll be able to be more generous with the faults of others. Then we can give praise to God and people alike.

Reflection Questions

Do you sometimes say mean things about others, even though you know you shouldn't? Could you try to find something positive to say instead?

_____

_____

_____

_____

Prayer

Lord, sometimes nasty things come out of my mouth. I know it's wrong. Please help me remember to say positive things or just keep my mouth quiet. Thank you for your perfect example! I love you! Amen.

DAY 71

DON'T PLAY FAVORITES

"My brothers and sisters, believers in our glorious Lord
Jesus Christ must not show favoritism."

JAMES 2:1

Jesus spent time with his disciples, but he also spent time with tax collectors, the most hated sinners in the cities. He did not show favoritism to anyone. He was kind and loving to all. If you say you're a follower of Jesus, then you must act like him.

Amanda and Kylie arrived at the lunch table at the same time. There was only one seat left. Amanda wasn't as popular, and her hand-me-downs didn't quite fit her. Kylie had the latest haircut and trendy clothes. "This seat is saved for Kylie," several girls said. Amanda, not surprised, went to look for another table. She'd just been the victim of favoritism.

Favoritism—unfair treatment because of discrimination or prejudice—is hurtful. The Bible clearly says that if you're a believer, you shouldn't show favoritism. Treat others the same, no matter how they are dressed or how much money they have. The reasons behind your actions determine whether you are showing favoritism or not. If you want to be friends with someone just because they're popular, then you're only being nice to get something. That's not love—that's greed. "If you give special attention and a good seat to the rich person, but you say to the poor one, 'You can stand over there, or else sit on the floor'—well, doesn't this discrimination show that your judgments are guided by evil motives?" (James 2:3-4 NLT).

It hurts to be the victim of favoritism. It makes you feel as if you're not worth as much as other people. But that's never true! We all are equal in God's eyes. He never plays favorites among his children.

Be like God. Treat others with equal love and care.

Reflection Questions

Have you ever been rejected because of what you didn't own? Have you ever rejected someone over what they didn't have? If so, ask for their forgiveness—and God's too!

_____

_____

_____

_____

Prayer

Lord, I should be what content with what I have, but it's hard. Please help me to remember that you are all I really need. I want to be as kind to others as you are to me. Thank you. Amen.

HEARING IMPAIRED

"Why didn't I pay attention to my instructors?
I have come to the brink of utter ruin,
and now I must face public disgrace."

PROVERBS 5:13–14 (NLT)

Someone at the end of his life spoke these words. When it was too late, he realized that the teachers in his youth had tried to help him learn valuable lessons for life. But he didn't pay attention, and instead he experienced total ruin: physically, financially, and socially. He was disgraced and ashamed. It could have been prevented if he'd listened to his teachers.

You have teachers at home (your parents and grandparents), at school (your instructors), and at church (Sunday school teachers, pastors, and youth leaders). They're all trying to help you learn valuable things so your life will be successful. Sometimes we feel these people are too old or too out of touch to be able to teach us what we need to know. They didn't grow up in our world, so how can they know what things to teach us?

Because some things never change. Principles for building loving relationships, gaining financial success through hard work, and taking care of our bodies don't change. Those principles are found in the Bible, and the Word of God is the same forever.

God's Word has some pretty strong words for people who won't listen to instruction and teaching. "The fear of the LORD is the beginning of knowledge, but fools despise wisdom and instruction" (Proverbs 1:7 NKJV). And "Whoever loves instruction loves knowledge, but he who hates correction is stupid" (Proverbs 12:1 NKJV).

Make up your mind to love instruction. Learn the principles that will lead to a successful, happy life.

Reflection Questions

Do you listen when your parents have something to talk about with you? Do you thank your parents for guiding you?

_____

_____

_____

_____

Prayer

Lord, I know you gave me my mom and dad and others to help guide me in your ways. Thank you for their help in my life. Please help me to remember that they love me and want what's best for me. Thank you. Amen.

147

Payback Time: A Tempting Trap

"Make sure that nobody pays back wrong for wrong, but always
strive to do what is good for each other and for everyone else."

1 THESSALONIANS 5:15

Christians aren't supposed to strike back when someone has
offended or wronged them. While hurt feelings may tempt you
to pay someone back for what she did, don't do it. Instead, as a
follower of Jesus, forgive her and try to be kind to everyone.

Sarah was hurt and angry when her best friend invited
another girl to spend the night, but didn't invite Sarah. On
Monday Sarah heard the other girl talking about all the fun
they'd had, going to a movie, ice skating, and making fudge.
Sarah fumed all week, even though she pretended that she didn't
mind. But Sarah wanted revenge. She intended to pay her friend
back by doing the same thing to her, only Sarah would make sure
she planned even MORE fun things to do.

Sarah had fallen into a tempting trap. Wanting revenge is
even worse than being stuck in hurt feelings. Sarah became bitter toward her friend, trying to wound her as much as she'd been
wounded. Sarah ended up killing the friendship.

God doesn't want that for you. When friends disappoint you,
go first to God with your hurt feelings. Ask for his help to forgive
your friend. Talk about it with a parent. Then go to your friend

and talk about the situation. There may be reasons for her actions you know nothing about.

Retaliation is never the Christian choice. Christians are called to forgive. "Do not say, 'I'll pay you back for this wrong!' Wait for the LORD" (Proverbs 20:22). Give up the idea of paying someone back. Let the Lord free you instead.

REFLECTION QUESTIONS

Have you ever wanted revenge when someone hurt you? What did you do about it? Did it help or make the situation worse? Did you talk to God about it?

_____

_____

_____

_____

PRAYER

Lord, getting revenge is so tempting. I know it's not right, and I need your help to let go and forgive. Please help me to follow your example. Thank you. Amen.

Settle Down

"Stop striving and know that I am God."

PSALM 46:10 (NASB)

When times are frightening and our world is falling apart, the Lord tells us to calm down. We are to stop spending so much energy on figuring out what to do. He says to be silent, to be still. Remember that he is almighty God, and he has everything under control.

Kaitlyn forgot to lock her locker, and now her new running shoes are missing. Her mom saved for weeks to buy those shoes! Kaitlyn runs to the principal's office first, but they aren't in the Lost and Found. She checks all the hallways and restrooms, hoping they've been tossed somewhere. She throws everything out of her locker onto the floor, hoping they are buried under the clutter. She's near tears. Now what is she going to do?

When you're upset or angry or in pain, it takes faith to be quiet and concentrate instead on God's power to save you. Stretch your faith muscle, and think on the good things of God and how he's solved your problems in the past. "Meditate within your heart on your bed, and be still" (Psalm 4:4 NKJV).

Part of being still and knowing that he is God is trusting in a good outcome. If God is permitting problems or a crisis into our lives, he has a purpose. And if we trust him through it, he will make it all work out for our good. "We know that in all things God works for the good of those who love him, who have been called according to his purpose" (Romans 8:28).

The next time a problem hits you, *stop*. Don't wear yourself out running around. Get quiet instead. Let God speak to you and help you.

REFLECTION QUESTIONS

When you're upset, how do you act? Do you panic and have outbursts, or do you talk to God? Don't waste energy on emotions that get you nowhere!

_____

_____

_____

_____

PRAYER

Lord, I sometimes panic when things go wrong. I want to be calm. Please help me go to you first for help and patience. Thank you for your perfect example. Amen.

LIVING TO LOVE

"We know and rely on the love God has for us. God is love.
Whoever lives in love lives in God, and God in them."

I JOHN 4:16

We know how much God loves us. We trust in that and lean on him. God is love! Believers live in God, and he lives in them. True followers reflect God's love by loving others.

Kate tried to be loving, but it was so hard. She told herself not to snap at her brother, but she still did it. She made lists—like New Year's resolutions—of nice things she was going to do. But more often than not, she didn't do them. She was trying to be loving in her own strength and finding it impossible.

Love is more than an emotion we feel toward another person or some kind act we do. To truly love is to have God work through our lives. If you're a believer, then God lives in you. And God *is* Love. So God is patient, God is kind, he does not brag, he endures things, he believes all things, he is full of hope, and God never fails. (See 1 Corinthians 13:4-8.) As we ask him to work in us and love others through us, we will begin to see the very same characteristics become true in our lives. God is Love, and that's why "Love never fails" (1 Corinthians 13:8 NKJV).

First John 3:16 (NLT) says, "We know what real love is because Jesus gave up his life for us. So we also ought to give up our lives for our brothers and sisters." You may never have to physically die for anyone, but loving others will cause other things in you to die. You may have to die to selfishness, a short temper, or backbiting—any habit that prevents you from truly loving others.

God lives in you. Lean on that love, and spread it to others!

Reflection Questions

How hard (or easy) is it for you to be loving? Do you have bad habits that need to die?

Prayer

Lord, I know that you are love. Help me to be more loving, just as you love me. Thank you for your perfect example. Amen.

LOVE IS PATIENT, AND NOT EASILY ANGERED

"Above all, love each other deeply, because love covers over a multitude of sins."

I PETER 4:8

Love is shown in actions. Instead of picking at people's every fault, try to look past them. No one is perfect, and love shows that by being patient with others' weaknesses.

Maria and Rebecca were good friends and partners on a science project. Maria liked to talk while she worked. Rebecca found this annoying because Maria made mistakes and wasted time that way. Rebecca mentioned it, and Maria tried to curb her talking. Sometimes she succeeded, but often she failed. Rebecca valued her friendship with Maria, so she chose not to nag her about it.

Rebecca is a good example of "covering over many sins." This verse is part of Peter's letter to Christians who are truly trying to improve their relationships with God and people. Even when we try hard, we will have failures. So will others. "Covering over a multitude of sins" means having a patient or tolerant attitude toward the mistakes of others. The aim of this verse is to avoid criticizing others for tiny faults or weaknesses.

However, this verse does NOT mean that you should cover

up serious sins or criminal acts, such as physical beatings and sexual abuse. Love expects responsible behavior from others. Covering up such acts allows the irresponsible person to continue their very wrong actions. Whether it is happening to you or to someone else, report it. Don't cover it up.

We all have minor faults and weaknesses we're trying to conquer. We appreciate it when others are kind to us and understand our failures. Give that same love and understanding to others.

Reflection Questions

Think of the friend you spend the most time with. Is there a habit of hers that you don't mention because you love her? Do you have any habits that she lovingly doesn't mention?

_____

_____

_____

_____

Prayer

Lord, I know I'm not perfect. Please help me to be loving in the way I deal with bad habits or something that bugs me. Help me to know if or when to say anything. Thank you for being the perfect model of love! Amen.

DAY 77

LEAN ON THE LORD

"Blessed is the man who trusts in the LORD,
And whose hope is the LORD."

JEREMIAH 17:7 (NKJV)

A girl who trusts in the Lord will be happy and full of blessings. Trusting the Lord includes leaning on and relying on the Lord—not people—for hope and self-confidence and acceptance.

Trust can be hard. Do you have trouble trusting other people? Have people mistreated you, or let you down, or broken their promises to you? Maybe they overlooked you when you needed attention. How did that make you feel? Being mistreated and ignored can make us overly sensitive later in life. If you feel destroyed emotionally when your friend doesn't compliment your new haircut, her opinion is too important. If you're depressed for weeks when someone doesn't invite you to a party, your hope is in the wrong place. You're using other people's reactions to you to define who you are. If you look to others to let you know if you're "okay" or "acceptable," you will constantly need to be working for their love and approval.

If you have learned to trust in other people for your self-worth, it's time to shift that trust to God. If we trust in him, we won't be let down. Even the most loving parents or devoted friends will let us down sometimes. They're human, not perfect. But believers can trust God for their self-esteem. We can count on him to see us through any pain or difficulty we're in. No matter how much you love other people, keep your total trust in God alone. "The LORD God, my God, is with you. He will not fail you nor forsake you" (1 Chronicles 28:20 NASB).

Trust in the Lord. Put your hope in him. He will never, *ever* let you down.

REFLECTION QUESTIONS

When you do something, do you think about what your friends will say? How often do you think about what God will say?

_____

_____

_____

_____

PRAYER

Lord, I know I put too much importance on what others think of me. Help me to think only of what you think of me. I want to be more like you. Thank you. Amen.

I'VE GOT THE JOY, JOY, JOY . . .

"Now I am coming to You; and I say these things [while I am still] in the world so that they may experience My joy made full and complete and perfect within them [filling their hearts with My delight]."

JOHN 17:13 (AMP)

Jesus is talking here to his Father, God, about his disciples. (If you're a believer, that's you too!) Jesus said he taught his followers how to live so they could be happy. Jesus wants you to have "gladness" filling your heart and joy flooding your soul.

Some days it's easy to feel joy. You get an A on a test. Your hair looks great. Your little brother is staying overnight with a friend. But what about the days you fall in the mud, you forget your homework, and you're grounded for doing something you shouldn't have? Can you have joy on those days? Believe it or not, yes, you can. Your joy comes from the Lord, not from your circumstances.

One reason Jesus wants you to be filled with joy is that he loves you. Another reason is that joy makes you strong! "Do not sorrow, for the joy of the LORD is your strength" (Nehemiah 8:10 NKJV). Satan delights in stealing your joy because a lack of joy also steals your strength and makes you weak. When you're weak, it's easier for him to tempt you and discourage you. When you're weak, you probably won't be sharing the good news with others either.

Understand this: *it is God's will for you to enjoy life!* "This is the day the Lord has made; we will rejoice and be glad in it" (Psalm 118:24 NKJV).

Reflection Questions

Who gets the credit when you have good days? Who do you usually blame for the bad days? How can you remember to have joy *every* day?

_____

_____

_____

_____

Prayer

Lord, I want to be filled with joy. Please show me anything
that Satan is using to steal my joy. I want to love my
life on good days and bad. Thank you. Amen.

159

When Trouble Comes

"I have told you these things, so that in me you may have
peace. In this world you will have trouble. But take heart! I
have overcome the world."

JOHN 16:33

Jesus overcame every trouble he encountered in his life on earth.
He even overcame death! If you're a believer, Jesus lives in you,
and you have this very same power. So you can be at peace, even
though you will face trials and sorrows in this life. Cheer up and
take courage!

Trouble comes in all shapes and sizes. You might have
people problems: your best friend is moving to a new city, or
there's a bully at school. You might have money troubles: you
can't afford to join your friends at the water park, or your family's
been evicted from your apartment for not paying the rent. The
size or the shape of your problem doesn't matter though. If Jesus
lives in you, you can overcome it.

Sometimes people are told that if they just accept Jesus as
their Savior, all their problems will be over. The Bible clearly
teaches that is not so. Jesus told his disciples that they *would*
have troubles, but not to be discouraged by them. They could
lean on him and overcome them. God uses the trials and tests in
our lives to teach us valuable things, like patience and endurance

and the power of prayer. We wouldn't develop these necessary qualities if life were smooth all the time.

Jesus said, "Peace I leave with you; my peace I give you. I do not give to you as the world gives. Do not let your hearts be troubled and do not be afraid" (John 14:27). So be at peace. Have courage. Then lean on God to help you overcome every trouble that comes your way.

REFLECTION QUESTIONS

When you talk to God about your problems, do you ask them to be taken away? Or do you ask God to help you through them?

_____

_____

_____

_____

PRAYER

Lord, it is tough to get through problems. Please give me patience and peace as I give my troubles to you. Thank you for always being with me. Amen.

WATCH WHERE YOU WALK

"Blessed is the one
   who does not walk in step with the wicked
or stand in the way that sinners take
   or sit in the company of mockers."

PSALM 1:1

You will have a happy life if you respect God's laws and obey them. But you must avoid arranging your life according to what unbelievers say. They laugh at God's laws and defiantly reject his ways. Don't take advice from such people. Don't even hang around with those who make sinful behavior a way of life.

Some of these people are easy to spot, and therefore easy to avoid. They sneer when you mention church. They swear using God's name as a curse word. They do whatever they please as their way of life.

However, some who reject God's laws aren't so easy to identify. Jill was bitter about her parents' divorce, and nothing her mom or dad could say made any difference. When she confided her hateful feelings to her best friend at church, her friend said, "What they did was terrible. Look how it's affected your life! You've had to move, your mom has no money, and you have to go back and forth all the time. If you forgive them, they'll think what they did is all right with you." Jill's friend meant well in her sympathy, but her advice classifies her as a "mocker." She is disrespecting much of God's Word that commands us to forgive (Matthew 6:14–15; 18:21–22; 2 Corinthians 2:7; and many more).

When situations come up, many voices will tell you what you should do. Listen to only the voice that tells you to obey God's written Word. When God's will becomes the most important thing to you—when you choose to follow God's Word and nothing else—the naysayers will no longer be walking with you.

Walk on the narrow path defined by God's Word, and watch how joyful your life becomes!

REFLECTION QUESTIONS

Who do you ask for advice? Are they Christians? Do they give the advice that God would give? Do you ask him directly for help?

_____

_____

_____

_____

PRAYER

Lord, I get all kinds of advice about everything.
Please help me to know whose advice to follow.
Help me to come to you first, always. Thank
you for always being there for me. Amen.

DAY 81

THE FREEDOM OF FORGIVENESS

"Forgive us our sins,
for we also forgive everyone who sins against us."

LUKE 11:4

When we forgive, we give the other person freedom, just as God gives us freedom from the shame and guilt of our own sins. When we forgive, we give up our "right" to pay someone back for what they did to us.

Kyla endured physical beatings when her dad would get drunk; they didn't stop until the school nurse spotted the bruises and reported it. A neighbor boy had been molesting Britney until her mom caught him and turned him over to the police. Should these girls forgive their abusers? Believe it or not, yes.

However, we need to understand what forgiveness is—and what it *isn't*. Forgiveness is NOT:

Pretending that something bad didn't happen.
Pretending that what happened wasn't so bad after all.
A quick shortcut to get rid of hurt feelings.

Forgiveness IS:

Letting go of getting even.

Putting the responsibility for what happened on the
wrongdoer's shoulders, where it belongs.
Giving your hurt to God so he can begin the healing.

It may take a long time, and you may need help to do it, but
(for your own sake) forgive the person who abused you.

Forgiveness does NOT make what they did to you okay. It
just means you have given up your right for revenge. You release
your hurt and bitterness, and you let God (and maybe the courts)
deal with that person.

Forgive—and set *yourself* free.

Reflection Questions

Do you have a bad experience that needs forgiveness? Do you har-
bor bad feelings toward someone? Have you asked God to heal you?

_____

_____

_____

_____

Prayer

Lord, you know I've been deeply hurt. Please help me
to forgive and let go of this hurt. I know it wasn't my
fault. Please heal me, Lord. Thank you. Amen.

FAITH IN HIS WORD

"We live by faith, not by sight."

2 CORINTHIANS 5:7

As Christians, we should base our actions and our lives on what we believe, not on what we can see with our eyes or experience with our senses. Instead of magnifying our circumstances, we should focus on the truth in God's Word.

Do you feel frustrated with your math homework? No matter how hard you try, the answers are wrong. Do you decide you just can't do it? Or are you in a relationship with an angry person? Have you decided that you can't help it if all your conversations turn into fights? That may be how you *feel*, but it's not what God's Word says.

Your homework is so hard you can't do it? Truth: "I can do all this through him who gives me strength" (Philippians 4:13). God's Word says you can lean on his strength and power to get the job done. Your conversations with that angry person have to end up in fights? Truth: "A gentle answer turns away wrath, but a harsh word stirs up anger" (Proverbs 15:1). God's Word says if you answer him with a gentle answer, it will soften his anger.

Are you going to believe what you see with your eyes and experience with your emotions? Or are you going to believe what God says in his Word? Remember, "God is not a man, that He should lie" (Numbers 23:19 NKJV). His Word is the absolute truth.

Your problems may not disappear overnight. God may seem slow in coming to the rescue, but he uses the waiting time to stretch your faith and encourage you to be steady in prayer. "We fix our eyes not on what is seen, but on what is unseen, since what is seen is temporary, but what is unseen is eternal" (2 Corinthians 4:18).

Trust God, and live according to your belief in him.

Reflection Questions

How often do you let your feelings rule your actions? Do you ever convince yourself of something because that's how you really "feel"?

_____

_____

_____

_____

Prayer

Lord, I let my feelings get the better of me sometimes. Please help me to go to you first. I want my actions to reflect you. Thank you. Amen.

What Goes Up, Must Come Down

"Those who exalt themselves will be humbled, and those who humble themselves will be exalted."

MATTHEW 23:12

You have two choices. You can praise and promote and honor yourself. If you do, your condition will be brought back down by force or by discipline. On the other hand, if you're willing to humble and restrain yourself, God will lift you up. He will honor you when the time is right.

Maddie bragged continually about her private voice lessons and told everyone she'd get the lead in the school musical. She was so sure she'd win the part that she started memorizing the heroine's lines. She said she hoped Leah got a chorus part because Leah's voice would make good background music for Maddie's solo. When the cast list was posted, however, Leah had the lead and Maddie was on the scenery crew. Maddie's voice was exceptional, but her attitude of superiority cost her the part she wanted.

Being puffed up with pride is a big deal with God. Pride turned Lucifer, a beautiful angel, into Satan, the devil. Being humble is being able to see yourself through God's eyes. Humility is not thinking you're a no-good worm. After all, we're made in God's very own image. But we are also to hold others up higher and not have an overly exalted opinion of ourselves. Pride and humility cannot live in the same heart. We can confess the pride and get rid of it. Or we can puff ourselves up with pride, and then endure the painful consequences when God corrects us. "Pride goes before destruction, and a haughty spirit before a fall" (Proverbs 16:18 NKJV).

Have a healthy self-esteem, but remain humble. Wait for God to lift you to a place of importance when the time is right. He will!

REFLECTION QUESTIONS

How often do you talk about yourself to others? Do you brag about your talents? Or do you give God the credit?

_____

_____

_____

_____

PRAYER

Lord, I know you have given me talents to use. Please help me to be humble and use my talents for your glory. Thank you for all that you see in me. Amen.

FOR ALL THE RIGHT REASONS

"Whatever you do, whether in word or deed, do it all in the name of the Lord Jesus."

COLOSSIANS 3:17

In the words you say or the things you do, remember that you represent the Lord. Say and do things for the right reasons, with godly motives.

Cara and Nicole were friends at church, and they both decided to babysit during the summer. Cara took care of two preschoolers while their single mom worked. This mom couldn't pay as much, but she let Cara take the children to summer Bible school. Nicole babysat for another family. They had a pool, money for ordering pizzas, and a big-screen TV. Nicole thought she'd have more fun working for this family. Which girl do you suppose is babysitting in the name of the Lord?

Why do you do the things you do? Why do you say the things you say? Is it because you want others to feel the love of God flowing through you to them? Or, if you look deeper, might you find another reason? Maybe you say a kind word or do a favor for someone to gain their approval, or so they won't be mad at you. (Would Jesus do it for those reasons?) Maybe you do something, like babysit for your aunt, because you feel like you have no choice. These are not good motives. Remember, "Whatever you do, do it heartily, as to the Lord and not to men" (Colossians 3:23 NKJV). Don't look to people for a reward for good deeds, but look to God to bless you.

Check your motives. Do the right things for the right reasons.

Reflection Questions

Why do you do things? Do you figure out what you can get out of it before you agree? Do you ask God what you can do for him?

_____

_____

_____

_____

Prayer

Lord, it's easy to do things for my benefit. Please help me to do things for your sake. I want to help others in order to lift you up, not me. Thank you for reminding me why I should do things. Amen.

DAY 85

RUN WITH JOY

"None of these things move me; nor do I count my life dear
to myself, so that I may finish my race with joy."

ACTS 20:24 (NKJV)

The apostle Paul had endured many hardships (beatings, ship-wrecks, imprisonment), yet he said those things didn't change his direction or purpose in life. He was even ready to die, if necessary. His only goal was to finish his race with joy.

You may not face a shipwreck or a prison sentence in your lifetime, but you'll face other things. It could be a teacher who likes to embarrass you. Or maybe you get teased about being the tallest girl in your class. Maybe you have a parent who is never satisfied with anything you do, no matter how hard you try. These are hardships too.

How could Paul finish his race with joy, when it was filled with hardships? His secret is found in 2 Corinthians 12:10: "That is why, for Christ's sake, I delight in weaknesses, in insults, in hardships, in persecutions, in difficulties. For when I am weak, then I am strong." How can that be possible? Because when Paul was weak, he leaned on God harder for help. He depended on God's strength to get the job done. And when you're filled with the strength of almighty God, that's strong!

So no matter what you're experiencing right now, you can

do what Paul did. If you're filled with God's strength, you'll feel joy in your life and work, a joy that can't be explained. And when you've accomplished what you set out to do, you'll be able to say like Paul: "I have fought the good fight, I have finished the race, I have kept the faith" (2 Timothy 4:7 NKJV).

Complete your race with joy!

Reflection Questions

How do you face hardships and problems? Do you grumble, or do you smile and praise God? It might be hard, but the prize at the end of this race is priceless!

_____

_____

_____

_____

Prayer

Lord, I know there will be times of trial in my life. Help me to stay joyful and remember that you're always with me. I want to depend only on you! Amen.

THE RIGHT FRIENDS MAKE ALL THE DIFFERENCE

"He who walks with wise men will be wise,
But the companion of fools will be destroyed."

PROVERBS 13:20 (NKJV)

If you make friends with those who exercise good judgment and common sense, you will learn to do the same. But if you choose fools for friends—those who lack good judgment—you will learn their ways instead. In the end, you will be defeated and ruined.

Before Amber moved, her closest friend, Carrie, lived next door. They studied together at night, and they quizzed each other before tests. They also ran a babysitting business and saved money to buy new bikes. At her new school, Amber's best friend was just as fun, but when they got together to study, Jasmine talked and flipped through fashion magazines or watched TV. Jasmine got a hefty weekly allowance, but it was always gone within a few days. Before long, Amber's grades slipped too. She cleaned out her savings account to buy clothes she didn't really want. Jasmine was a nice girl, but not a wise one. By being close friends with Jasmine, Amber had learned her undisciplined ways.

Some foolish friends are openly defiant as well. They cheat on their homework, they lie to their parents about where they're going, and they steal money from their dads' wallets. Avoid friends like this too! "Let no one deceive you with empty words, for because of such things God's wrath comes on those who are disobedient. Therefore do not be partners with them" (Ephesians 5:6–7).

Friends are one of God's greatest blessings in this life. They are meant to be enjoyed and treasured. However, you must choose your friends with care!

Reflection Questions

Think about your closest friends. Would God approve of how they live their lives? What do you do when you're with them?

_____

_____

_____

_____

Prayer

Lord, having friends is important to me. Having friends who love and act like you is even more important. Please help me to see their true colors. Thank you. Amen.

RIDING THE WAVES

> "When you ask, you must believe and not doubt, because the one who doubts is like a wave of the sea, blown and tossed by the wind. That person should not expect to receive anything from the Lord."
>
> JAMES 1:6–7

In some hurtful or confusing situations, we don't know what to do. There isn't always a specific Bible verse that spells out our answer. However, we can always go to God for wisdom. You must believe in your heart that God hears you and will answer you. People who can't make up their minds—believing one minute, then doubting the next—are as unstable as the rolling waves of the sea. People like that should not expect to receive anything from the Lord.

Do you doubt God when a fearful thought crosses your mind? Satan tries to attack all believers with doubt. To know if you're really "double-minded," check what's coming out of your mouth. Do you sound like this? "I prayed to God, but I don't know. It's taking a long time to get my prayer answered. I don't think God heard me or will help me." THAT'S doubt.

The one who gets her prayers answered, the Bible says, is the one who prays in faith. And after a time, when nothing seems to be happening, the words coming out of her mouth are still filled with faith: "I know God heard me. I know my answer is on its way. God's timing is perfect. He won't be late by a single hour." That's what faith is—believing even before circumstances match up. "Without faith it is impossible to please Him, for he who comes to God must believe that He is, and that He is a rewarder of those who diligently seek Him" (Hebrews 11:6 NKJV).

Believe God—and keep believing—when you pray. He'll never let you down.

Reflection Questions

Do you ask God for help and leave your troubles in his hands? Or do you ask for help, but do your own thing anyway because you think it's better?

Prayer

Lord, I know I don't always wait for your answer.
Please help me to have patience and to trust
that you will come through for me. You always
have; you always will! Thank you. Amen.

NOTHING BUT THE TRUTH

"Do not lie to one another, since you stripped off the old self with its evil practices."

COLOSSIANS 3:9 (NASB)

The message of this verse is simple: do not lie to one another. It doesn't fit who you are now. You've done away with your old self with its morally wrong practices.

Kylie paused the movie when her phone buzzed. It was a text from Darla, the boring girl who lived two doors down, asking if she wanted to come over and swim in the pool. "Sorry, I can't," Kylie wrote back. "I'm stuck doing chores." She felt a twinge of guilt, but lying seemed better than spending time with Darla or telling her she was boring.

Most of us think of ourselves as honest people, yet even some people who identify themselves as believers lie many times each day. Why do we do it, when we know that lying is wrong? Sometimes we don't want to be held responsible, so we hide behind made-up excuses. "I didn't have time to do it. I've been too busy!" Or we lie to avoid discipline: "I didn't know it was due *today*." Or we want to look good in front of someone else: "Oh yeah, I love that movie." (Even though you've never even heard of it.)

Why is telling the truth so important in loving others?

Because telling the truth builds trust, and lies destroy trust.

Love and lies don't mix. If you love someone, you will tell them the truth. Telling the truth takes courage and confidence. It means taking a risk that someone will reject you for owning up to your failures or fears. Being completely honest isn't easy, but God's Word is clear: do not lie.

You're a new person now. Build trust with others by being truthful.

Reflection Questions

Think of the last time you told a little white lie. Do you think it solved the problem, or did it make the problem last longer? What could have been the benefit of telling the truth? What does God say to do?

_____

_____

_____

_____

Prayer

Lord, sometimes little lies seem to solve problems for me. Please help me to remember that the truth spoken in love is so much better than lying. I want to be a good model of you. Thank you. Amen.

DAY 89

Pursue Peace

"We pursue the things which make for peace and the building up of one another."

ROMANS 14:19 (NASB)

We are to pursue the things that lead to peace and building one another up. *Pursue* is a strong word, meaning "to search, hunt for, or go after." Sometimes it takes hard work to live in peace with people, but we are commanded to make every effort to do so.

In Megan's history class, each student had to choose a person in history for an oral report presentation. Carrie discovered that Megan had chosen Rosa Parks, the same person she was reporting on. She got upset and ran to the teacher, demanding that Megan choose another historical figure. Megan was then called to the teacher's desk. She listened to Carrie's complaint, but she'd already done a lot of research for the report herself. Yet, she knew she should make an effort to find a peaceful solution. "We could choose different parts of Rosa Parks's life to report on," Megan suggested, "and then we could still use the same person." Carrie frowned and said, "Well, I get to report on how she refused to give up her seat on the bus." Megan nodded and said, "Okay. I have some books about that, if you want them. I'll cover her childhood in my report."

"Behold, how good and how pleasant it is for brethren to

dwell together in unity!" (Psalm 133:1 NKJV). Seeking peace and pursuing solutions that build up someone else will cost you something—usually having your own way. Choose your battles, the things you feel you must fight for. Few things are worth an all-out war.

Instead, "Encourage each other and build each other up, just as you are already doing" (1 Thessalonians 5:11 NLT). God will reward you for it.

Reflection Questions

When you have a conflict with someone, how do you react? Do you need to win? Do you try to find a peaceful solution?

_____

_____

_____

_____

Prayer

Lord, it's hard to always keep the peace. I need your help
to stay calm and find peaceful ways of doing things.
Please help me stay humble. Thank you! Amen.

DAY 90

DON'T WORRY: PRAY

"Don't worry about anything; instead, pray about everything."

PHILIPPIANS 4:6 (NLT)

As believers, we are not to be anxious or upset, troubled or uneasy in our minds. How? Pray about everything, and turn the situations over to God for help.

What do you catch yourself worrying about? Starting at a new school? How much your skin is breaking out? What your friends really think of you? Whether your parents' fighting is going to end in divorce? Whatever your worries are—no matter how big—the answer is to pray instead of worry. Easier said than done, right? Well, try these ways to tame that worry habit:

Separate unhelpful, needless worry from real concerns.
Decide if you can do anything about the situation. If so, write down a plan to handle it.
Don't worry alone. Talk to a friend, parent, teacher, youth leader, or counselor. You may receive helpful advice.
Take care of your body. We are more likely to worry when we're too tired, aren't eating healthy meals, and aren't getting enough exercise.
Try to look on the bright side. There is good in nearly every situation or person. Think of some things you're grateful for right now, and focus on them.

Control your imagination. Don't get distracted by what-ifs. Our imaginations can take us from mild worry to a full-blown anxiety attack if we don't choose more realistic thoughts. Stick to what's happening right now—not what might happen in the future.

Trust God. Whatever situation you're facing, invite God into the middle of it. You and God make an unbeatable team!

Worrying is a bad habit, but trusting God can become a habit too. So bring your worries to him, and live a life filled with peace.

REFLECTION QUESTIONS

When you have a worry, what do you tend to do? Does worry take over your life, or do you give it to God and get on with living?

_____

_____

_____

_____

PRAYER

Lord, there's always something to worry about. Please help me to come to you first, giving you all my concerns. Thank you for always taking care of me. Amen.

A Little More Space

"And pray in the Spirit on all occasions with all kinds of prayers and requests. With this in mind, be alert and always keep on praying for all the Lord's people."

EPHESIANS 6:18

God loves you and cares about what's happening in your life. Here is a little more space to help you get to know God better. Jot down your thoughts, your prayers, your worries, favorite Bible verses, the names of friends you're concerned about—any and all of it! Writing it down will help draw you closer to God and strengthen your relationship with him. Come to him with all your heart!

....

....

....

....

....

....

....